I0812285

WELCOME TO THE VEGEDOME!

LAURA LEE FLANAGAN, PHD, ESQ.

hardcore vegetarian

WELCOME TO THE VEGEDOME!

EDITED: Nancy Mendelson
PHOTOGRAPHY: Bibs Carlsen and Laura Lee Flanagan
ILLUSTRATIONS: Deborah Bassino

PROCESS

This book about cooking is dedicated to my cousin Tom Scott (1948–2023) and porcini mushrooms…a visceral conversation about which was the last one we had just a day before he died.

Tom was a tremendous cook and the first person who inspired me to experiment with unfamiliar herbs and spices. He was a master of Indian and Thai and Chinese cuisines, and I am forever grateful to have eaten so much of his wonderful food, and to have known him.

He enriched my life.

During the last few years, Tom learned to make bagels. As it turns out, they were the best bagels I have ever tasted. Go figure…an Australian immigrates to the U.S., winds up in Kingston, MA, and makes the best bagels this New York native has ever eaten.

table of contents

prologue

FOOD = LOVE

Food is a primal expression of love. I feel blessed to have been raised in a home where food was just that, and nothing more. I was not taught to associate it with good or bad body image or social requirements and didn't have the opportunity to divert myself with junk that charades as food. I thank my mother eternally for this understanding.

Food is what we build our bodies with. It becomes the structure that allows us to do everything else we want to and have to do in this life. The idea of putting garbage into our bodies is anathema to me. I want my structure strong so I can go out and live!

The food that I make, I make with love. And Harley always notes that it all tastes so much better because of this. I make food for people as an expression of love. I want them to be well, to have sustenance, and then some—to be nourished and healthy and then experience the pleasure of good food as a bonus.

I hope you enjoy the recipes in this book. I hope you have or learn to have an appreciation for food and the amazing gifts we can give ourselves and the people we love every day. It's all about choices, and we have so many. *Buon appetito a tutti!*

introduction

My mother is Italian. I'm an Italian citizen; I lived in Italy. I was raised with a deep reverence for food and the practices and traditions that surround cooking and eating, family, process, creativity. I respect food and love everything about it…except cleaning up.

I am lucky to have married the love of my life, a man often caught saying, "I wish I didn't have to eat at all"; he would have been happy to drink his sustenance or just take a pill.

MADNESS!

Over the years I have learned that Harley really loves food and I really love to cook for him. In this way, as in so many ways, we bring balance to each other's lives. As a vegetarian, I think he spent so many years struggling to find delicious and healthy food, and so was content to simply take what he could get.

To release his latent foodie, I have enjoyed learning how to cook for a vegetarian and, in the process, have become a primarily plant-based pescatarian. I love concocting my own kinds of "fusion" dishes, blending Spanish and Greek or Thai and Indian, and experimenting with vegetarian ingredients in traditionally meat-centric dishes and making it work…and deliciously!

One of the richest vegetarian cuisines is Indian. Cooking Indian food was very intimidating to me because I was unfamiliar with the spices. But over time, I have learned to use Indian spices with the same confidence and creativity that I have always used Italian ones, and you can too.

Culturally, we are moving toward plant-based diets, but individually I know this can be daunting. Humans don't generally like change, and food is so entrenched in emotion and culture and family, and there is no doubt that "traditions" are some of the hardest behaviors to alter. But I have learned that so much of what I do now when I cook is to "tweak" foods I truly love, transforming them from meat-based to plant-based. And I have learned that removing the meat does not mean removing flavor or texture or satisfaction. If you give it some time, I believe you will not miss the meat; I definitely do not.

Hardcore Vegetarian has turned out to be a uniquely creative journey, one which I never would have expected…*kind of like being married.*

One of the first things Harley taught me, and it stays in my head to this day, is that non-vegetarians always try to feed vegetarians side dishes—and one cannot live on side dishes alone. The obvious scenario is Thanksgiving. If there is a vegetarian or a vegan at the table, they normally will be relegated to eating roasted or mashed potatoes, green beans, stuffing (if someone was thoughtful enough to make some outside the bird with vegetable stock), and yams, maybe a lucky salad. And that is just not enough substance. Vegetarians need a main course too!

Though I still eat fish, it is limited, and I maintain a primarily plant-based diet. I used to call myself a "lazy vegetarian"—meaning I kind of fell into it because I didn't want to make two dinners. But I do recall realizing a few years ago that I hadn't eaten "meat" in many years and was surprised…mostly because I didn't miss it at all.

That said, it was hard for me at the beginning to get out of the "side dish" mode. I had to really consider what I was preparing and learn new ways to think about it. So, going plant-based is indeed a thoughtful process, as I have mentioned. When Harley first started eating this way, his options were so limited. The good news is that today, there are so many choices for vegans and vegetarians—virtually every restaurant has some option and the number of vegan options in stores is insane.

In fact, we recently started to reduce our dairy intake in a significant way by using nut milks and yogurts and certain cheese substitutes. Although we're not totally there yet, many of these options are delicious and widely available. It's clear that a 100% plant-based diet is in our future. And just as energy companies have started to embrace green energy and invested in its development, so too have many of the big players in the food industry. It seems inevitable at this point.

If I can give any advice about the process of going plant-based, it is simply this: Don't beat yourself up and don't make it all or nothing. Deprivation does nothing but cause stress and emotional eating, which gets us nowhere. Start slow and gradually alter what you eat in increments. I think you will enjoy the food so much you will forget about meat, and then suddenly you will realize like I did, "wow, it's been years since I ate meat!"

I remember when Cro-Mags were touring the States one of the first times in the '80s… back then there were obviously not a lot of vegetarian options at any of the supermarkets or any of the restaurants, especially when you're outside any big city like New York, or L.A. or San Francisco. It starts getting difficult to get vegetarian food, at least it was back then—at best, like when we were in Chicago, we would get stuffed pizza or whatever, but there were not a lot of options. That being said, a lot of times on our long drives, me and John, and Doug too I guess, because Doug was not eating meat, we would make these sandwiches which were pretty much everything on bread that wasn't meat—so you'd wind up with a sandwich that had green peppers, red pepper, tofu, peanut butter, sprouts and pretty much everything that you could put on bread and eat. And it wasn't really about the taste as much as it was about putting food in your body because your body needs food in it; you're a machine, you need fuel. So, it wasn't like you were eating for taste; but it didn't suck that bad, and you got used to it—and sometimes you'd have cheese on 'em too. Again, you did not have any fake meat options or any vegan options, or any sort of protein drinks like that available in gas stations or supermarkets. —HF

step #1

FOOD FOR THOUGHT

Who Cares About Being Vegetarian?

Food has become political. To me that's weird. We've all got to eat, and we all want to be as healthy as we can be while we are wearing these bodies (if we care about staying alive and are rational), but tradition and culture are extremely powerful human systems, and physical habits require effort to change. Together, these work hard to prevent us from changing how we eat and how we live, and changing how we live becomes political. And oh yeah, there is our fast food, fake news, social nonsense culture…that doesn't help us either. We live in a culture that doesn't respect much, and food is low on the list.

Quality food (like quality work, ideas, and creativity) often requires time. Feeding people you love, including yourself, and caring about what they consume. takes more time than our culture wants us to spend on it… especially when we could be checking Instagram, scrolling through Reddit or entranced by TikTok.

There are many reasons to eat more plants and less meat. You know them. But I want to suggest that changing your diet, a habit, a tradition, requires all the thought and care that I described above. Taking the first steps to cook plant-based foods means you are thinking and caring and slowing down (as learning requires). And whether you become a vegetarian or a vegan in the end is up to you—no judgement here. If you simply cut back on meat consumption and experience the delicious and varied possibilities of plant-based foods, you will have already changed the habit. You will be caring, holistically, about consumption (food or information or products), which I believe leads to a healthier life in general.

OXO
Carmencita
ORGANIC BLACK PEPPERCORNS MILL

FIRST THINGS FIRST

Food Tips I Live By:

1. If you can buy organic and local, buy organic and local.
2. Eat and use as few processed foods and ingredients as possible (in other words, use/eat whole foods).
3. Don't be afraid of spices you haven't used before or grains that look intimidating.
4. Try to grow some fresh herbs and spices, even in the city by a window.

Kitchen "Must-Haves" to do this Right

Years ago, Harley took me to Patel Brothers in Jackson Heights, Queens, to load up on all sorts of Indian and Southeast Asian spices. But if Jackson Heights is not on the itinerary, and you're a spice novice like I was, I suggest you try "Shanti's Spice Box" as a great starting place; you can get it on Amazon.

For people who are interested in becoming vegetarian or tipping the scale to a more plant-based diet, Indian is a great way to go. And even though the cuisine is filled with so many vegetarian options, I have found that many dishes I once enjoyed with meat can easily become vegetarian without missing a thing. It's all about the spice.

I know that many people do not love Indian spices; however, do not despair, the world is filled with extraordinary vegetarian possibilities from Thai to Italian and everything in between. I especially love concocting my own kinds of "fusion" dishes like blending Spanish and Greek or Thai and Indian. Don't be afraid to experiment...remember, if it doesn't work, you can always get take-out!

Don Wapo
Cro-Mags
"Age of Hot Sauce"

I TRY TO KEEP THE FOLLOWING ITEMS IN MY KITCHEN AT ALL TIMES:

ESSENTIAL DRIED SPICES / DRIED HERBS

SHORT LIST MUST-HAVES

Whole black pepper*
Himalayan salt (grinder)
Sea salt*
Variety of salts (black, pink, kosher)
Chile powder*
Red pepper powder
Crushed red pepper*
Jalapeño powder
Turmeric powder*
Oregano*
Parsley
Rosemary*
Thyme
Garlic powder*
Cumin*
Garam masala
Sage
Mild Madras curry powder*
a couple of different curry blends
  (Indian, West African, Thai)

FRESH HERBS

Basil*
Italian parsley (flat leaf)*
Chives
Cilantro*
Sage
Rosemary

OIL, VINEGAR AND SAUCES

High-quality extra virgin olive oil
  (for dipping, drizzling)
Light olive oil
  (better at high temps)*
Vegetable/peanut oil
  (best for frying)*
Toasted sesame oil*
Coconut oil*
White truffle oil*
Soy sauce*
Hoisin sauce
Teriyaki sauce
Fish sauce (vegetarian fish sauce)*
Coconut milk (light and regular)*
High-quality aged balsamic vinegar
  (for dipping, drizzling)
Balsamic vinegar (for dressings)*
Red wine vinegar
White wine or champagne vinegar
Rice wine vinegar
Apple cider vinegar*

SUNDRIES, GRAINS, AND FLOURS

Corn/chickpea flour*
Rye flour
Corn starch*
  organic/non-GMO
  all-purpose flour*
Egg substitute/egg replacer*
Pink lentils*
French lentils*
Couscous*
Dried pasta*
Wild rice*
Basmati rice*
Jasmine rice
Arborio or carnaroli rice*
Sesame seeds*
Fennel seeds*
Pignoli nuts*
Garbanzo beans (chickpeas)*
Black beans*
Borlotti beans (cranberry beans)

REFRIGERATED AND FROZEN STAPLES

Lemon juice* (from lemons if possible,
  bottled if not)*
Lime juice* (from limes if possible,
  bottled if not)*
Best quality aged Parmigiano-
  Reggiano or Grana Padano*
Best quality Pecorino Romano
  and/or Asiago
Frozen peas*
Frozen fresh pasta
Frozen fresh bread*
Plain yogurt (almond or coconut
  yogurt)*
Plain firm tofu*
Plain medium firm tofu
Naan
Hot sauce (all kinds: Mexican*,
  Thai*, Tabasco etc.)

VEGETABLE STOCK

I make my own vegetable stock and freeze it. I use it constantly, so I keep one container in the fridge and one in the freezer. I love making my own because I use all the vegetable scraps I accumulate while cooking, so I waste as little as possible. Whatever I slice off, snip, peel—broccoli stalks, outer fennel or onion skin, tough asparagus ends, pepper cores—I use it all. Of course, I make sure it is clean, and then I simply refill a bag that I keep in the freezer every time I cook. Pretty much once each week, on a Sunday—old school—I fill a pot with water, dump in a bunch of frozen veggies, add pepper and a little salt, a dried bay leaf or two and boil until reduced to a dark or light color. Some things call for a lighter stock and some darker. We eat a lot of maitake mushrooms. When I clean them, I cut off the harder stalk/base. The mushrooms make the stock very rich and dark, and the flavor is wonderful. I am sure other wild mushrooms would do the same.

After boiling it to the color I want, I let it cool in the pot. When cool enough, I strain out all the veggies and pour the stock into containers for storage or freezing. It will stay in the freezer for months, but it never gets that far; I always use it within weeks of making it. If you can compost, the veggie bits at the end of the boiling are perfect for that.

NOTE: I add very little salt to the stock because I will add more if needed when I use it in a recipe…always easier to add than take away ;)

RANDOM THOUGHTS ON SEASONAL FOOD AND SLOWLY GOING PLANT-BASED

Harley always makes fun of me because whenever I describe a dish that I think is made perfectly, I invariably use the word "simple." He smiles as that word is about to come out of my mouth, and sometimes says it with me. Then I punch his arm—it's kind of a "thing" at this point. To me "simple" means unobstructed by too many sauces or spices or condiments. Don't get me wrong, I love spicy dishes and rich curries and sauces, but nothing makes me happier than a "simple" piece of grilled or roasted anything, pretty much. Olive oil, sea salt, maybe a little garlic—that's it.

We are very lucky to have a year-round farmers market just two blocks from our apartment. But you would be surprised how many are peppered throughout urban and rural areas all over the place, with many local farms having their own or cooperative farm stands. Search your area. This is by far the best way to eat seasonal foods as well as eating local (cutting transportation and pollution attendant to traveling foods) and supporting the farms that are local to your area.

Eating whole, local, and more often than not, organic foods has become much easier these days and it's an "everybody wins" situation. That being said, I know there are some "food deserts" out there, and if you can find higher quality items there, they are almost always more expensive. As with all things in life, do the best with what you have while striving to improve. That goes for food as well. If your grocery store is the

only place to find fresh vegetables, try to buy seasonal ones; it is more likely they will not have traveled so far. If you have farmers markets and/or farm cooperatives, check them out, see what is available and affordable. You can start going plant-based on a budget that makes sense for you.

I realize that the vegetable bounty in Minnesota in January is challenging. I don't know how to ice fish. Just do your best to eat local. You'll be supporting local growers, and your food will be fresher.

SPRING

Ahhh, spring in New York. It really is especially lovely here in spring. The air is warmer, the trees are budding, the little baby birds are hopping around, and the farmers market is ALIVE—finally. Just when you thought you were becoming a squat brown tuberous vegetable…the asparagus shows up! And the fiddlehead ferns and and and…you get it.

Spring, in my opinion, is a period of reinvention. I get excited about cooking once again because suddenly my options blossom. By the time spring rolls around I am delighted to leave behind winter's heavier foods and soups, when I find myself relying more on Grubhub out of sheer boredom.

SUMMER

And GO! Summer is very special for plant-based people. It is as if you can't cook enough or fast enough to keep up with the abundance, and anyone lucky enough to have a vegetable garden knows all about that. What do I do with all my tomatoes? Anyone want a few extra pounds of zucchini? It is veggie madness! Speaking of tomatoes, you'll notice that I ask primarily for cherry tomatoes in my recipes. I find them more reliably flavorful. That said, you're welcome to substitute other types of tomatoes if you prefer.

If you are working on eating more plants this is a great time of year to start. Summer is the time to indulge in all the different vegetable options and start to de-emphasize meat because, well, you just don't need it. AND, with the vegetables as fresh and flavorful as they are in summer, you usually don't need more than a little olive oil and sea salt and you are in business, no matter how you are preparing your food.

That said, it is also hot, and who wants to sweat in the kitchen? I think we would all rather be outside grilling, so I try to keep my summer indoor recipes minimally heat-producing for less suffering.

FALL

Season of mists and mellow fruitfulness...
— "To Autumn" (John Keats)

OK, I am not trying to be a pretentious dick, but when I was in high school, I was a John Keats junkie...yup, true, and the rest is history. Indulge me—the fact is, he described autumn pretty damn well, and the rich abundance of the season is not just a visual feast but a culinary one as well.

Fall is a weird season because we are leaving the super-abundant rapture of summer with its endless variety. All of a sudden, we are seeing squash and gourds and pumpkins, and for the most part, people feel intimidated by them. And to the fearful, I say this: DON'T FEAR FALL SQUASH! They can be intimidating, I agree, but there are so many wonderful varieties, and they taste so different and delicious on their own or incorporated into recipes. Just start by carefully splitting, scooping out the seeds and "guts," rub with olive oil and a little sea salt and roast. See what happens—I think you will be pleased. All throughout the fall I serve some sort of squash as a side dish with whatever I am making.

Some you can eat the skin and others you cannot, so learn a bit about the different types. My favorites are delicata, acorn, butternut, kabocha, calabaza...even plain old pie pumpkin is lovely!

*And they are fabulous in soup—see soup recipes below.

WINTER

In the spirit of cooking with foods that are fresh in each season, winter can seem like the hardest because the "bounty" is limited, and without meat, even more so. But when I think of the number of roasted vegetables, and stews and curries that are so warm and inviting in the winter months, it doesn't seem so bad at all.

Root vegetables are the stars of winter cooking, and despite their humble looks, their flavors are beautifully distinct and surprising. Rutabaga, for example, which I used to use for its amazing flavor in chicken soup, is wonderful roasted or puréed with potatoes for a beautiful variation on mashed potatoes.

Note on winter variations: Any vegetable that you can roast, you can also make into purée or soup, you can toss them with pasta, or even create a risotto. Take them as the basics, then toss in some fresh crunchy scallions or chopped fresh herbs (Italian parsley always elevates everything it touches) and suddenly you have invented a new wonderful dish, congratulations! That's what I do. And don't be afraid to fail—plant-based "fails" are not as bad as meat fails *in my humble opinion.*

PLANT-BASED AT A SNAIL'S PACE

I have spoken about this before, but I think it is important to reiterate because food is so primal and wrapped up with basic human emotions. Like all good lasting habits, they either come early or we learn them over time and with some effort later in life. Eating well is no different.

We may have very important, meaningful memories of some things that are really bad for us; those are hard attachments to change. Food has that power because so many important life moments are tied to food—and let's not forget survival itself.

This is why it is important to go easy and be gentle with yourself. If you know you want to stop eating certain foods or in a certain way, slowly and incrementally make those changes. I think "cold turkey" only works if you are in real danger with the substance or habit—when your life is at imminent risk. For behavioral changes—"lifestyle changes"—set your goals and then move toward them in a slow, thoughtful way so each step becomes a habit, not a "diet." You are far more likely to succeed.

In an effort to be less abstract, I would suggest the following: If you eat meat every day, or five or six times each week, actively plan a couple of days to go meatless. And make it fun—pick a recipe or a cuisine or restaurant that you really are excited to try and just do it. Make the effort. And if you do it and enjoy it and feel happy with what you ate or cooked or the happiness others you love experienced, you will do it again. That is rewarding. And if you are rewarded for the new behavior, you will do it again...and hopefully again and again and again until you wake up one day and don't remember the last time you ate meat or junk food, or high fructose corn syrup—and don't miss it at all.

THE PROTEIN HYPE

In my lifetime I have been conscious of so many food fads. My parents never had weight issues, and my mother has one of those envious conditions where she can eat like a little piglet and is thin and fit and wears clothes that fit her at 18! Unfair and cruel...but true.

As you now know, I like whole foods. The more processed, the less likely I am to buy it. Early in our relationship Harley and I hit a tofu wall—it seemed like tofu was the only viable "protein" I could work with, given that I was afraid of all the packaged gluten-based meat substitutes, the taste of seitan, and all the insanely processed teriyaki, chorizo or Italian-flavored faux meats out there. I thought they were "gross," and still more complicated for me was reading the ingredients and then trying to adapt what I was cooking to the flavors they already added. I even tried to make my own gluten-based fake meat at one point (that was a fail).

Since living with Harley, it's been all about "protein." In fact, I can't believe that restaurants ask people's choice of "protein"—as if it is some required component of the meal that must be added, as if nothing else in the food we eat supplies a sufficient amount of protein. With just a little bit of legwork, you can learn all about protein and how it is absorbed by your body and how much you actually need to maintain good health. Guess what: you are getting it from many different sources, not just meat and dairy. I won't get on a soap box, but some might say there is a lot of misinformation disseminated by various interested parties in the food industry.

But like all information tied to money (and most is), take it in critically and dig a little deeper. After all, this is your body you are feeding, and for now we still need it in order to get through life.

It is undeniable in my experience that, generally, vegetarians and vegans are healthier and in better physical condition than meat eaters. They also have fewer issues with inflammation and certainly do not suffer as widely from the most common first-world conditions like high cholesterol, blood pressure and heart disease. To me this is simple biology—Biology 101. We have long gastrointestinal tracts. Not as long as a cow or a straight herbivore, but WAY longer than a carnivore like a dog or a cat. A dog can eat in the morning, and that morning meal is in the park by the afternoon. People are not similarly equipped. Our food travels a great distance before it leaves our bodies and often sits around, slowly traveling. All organic matter breaks down within a period of time, and meat, as it decomposes, releases toxins that are not so good for us. The longer it takes to leave the body, the worse it is. Our bodies were made to pivot. It is a feature of our remarkable ability to survive and adapt that we can eat anything if we need to, in order to survive. But plants don't release the types of dangerous toxins that meat does over the time it takes for us to digest them.

If you do choose to do some homework, you will find the science is all over the place—but guess what, your body will tell you what's right. That might sound trite, but I think it is common sense. Our bodies tell us a lot, but our lives have so much noise in them that it is hard to hear or pay attention. Eat less chemically processed foods, number one. Animals and animal foods have a lot of fat in them that is not great for our health, and it shows up in our blood. Eat less of it and you will feel the difference and see the difference. And again, it is not all or nothing. Many studies say that eating meat only once a week, for example, will make all the difference in the world. The famed "Mediterranean Diet" is essentially plant-based with limited amounts of meat and fish, and it is considered one of the healthiest diets in the world, and people live long, healthy lives eating that way.

It's a process: just start slow, with things that taste good to you. Sustainability is the key to success (in all things, I find). If you can sustain it, it will not be a hassle and you will keep doing it; that is true for exercise and diet as well.

step #2

COURSES: IT'S ABOUT TIME

I have organized the main courses by the time required to prepare them. Time is the most valuable thing we have so I like the idea of being conscious of how we use it. Some recipes are fast, and some are slow—but I promise I will only include slow ones that are worth your precious time.

I. Main Courses

II. Soups and Salads

III. Sides and Small Plates

IV. Sweets

V. Random Thoughts on Seasonal Eating

VI. Epilogue: The Life-Altering Grilled Cheese

NOTE ON MEAT SUBSTITUTES: There are so many meat and dairy substitutes available these days; it is really an abundant time to be vegan or vegetarian. When Harley was a kid it was fries, pizza, bagels, and the Hare Krishnas. Meat substitutes are now available in all major grocery stores and specialty stores. Harley and I have developed our own choices, and I also consulted with an amazing vegan cook for her suggestions as well. That being said, not all substitutes are made equally; in fact, some are only available regionally, and quite frankly, some are made with ingredients I would not otherwise consume. I urge you to try different ones, read the ingredient labels and integrate as you choose (or not). There are many cuisines in the world that are completely vegetarian and have been for centuries, no faux meat required.

TOFU PREP: I use a lot of tofu and usually (but not always) prep it in some way first before I add it to the mix. A great basic preparation if you are not marinating it for hours before use (which is sometimes too much planning for me): remove it from the water and cut in half lengthwise. With a clean dishtowel or paper towels, wrap it and set it on a plate for a good half-hour to an hour so a lot of the moisture comes out.

Then sprinkle or rub with salt and pepper and whatever dominant seasoning you're cooking with (hot pepper mix, curry, garlic powder etc.). Cut into small cubes. Heat peanut oil very hot in a nonstick frying pan, and once a drop of water splatters in the pan, cook very high, flipping periodically so the tofu gets crunchy and browned. This takes around 15 minutes. Once done, remove from the pan with a slotted tool to leave the oil—and I set it on a plate with paper towels or dish towel on the bottom to drain some more oil.

BEANS: Beans are a vegetarian's friend. I love finding fresh borlotti (cranberry) beans at the farmers market—popping the beans out of their pods, each one a slightly different color. Dried beans are easy and faster to cook nowadays with the convenience of Instant Pots. But I realize most people are used to using canned beans. Canned beans are certainly time-saving when preparing multi-step meals. With this in mind, most of my recipes can be made with canned beans, unless fresh is specifically called for. You can always substitute dried as well.

NOTES ON DAIRY SUBSTITUTES: Harley and I are not vegans; we eat cheese, but Harley does not eat eggs. Most of the recipes in this book can be made vegan, and for each recipe, I will explain what to substitute.

VEGAN CHEESE: As we are not vegans, when cheese is called for in a recipe, I will make it with cheese. That said, we are slowly limiting the amount of cheese and dairy that we eat, and we often eat at vegan restaurants and regularly eat dairy substitutes. To give you the best choices I have asked my friend Alison Burney, an excellent vegan chef, to give you her best suggestions as well. The critical ones for the foods in this book are listed below but the list is by no means exhaustive; you should experiment:

Parmigiano Reggiano: *Parmesan by Angel Food* — it is good but salty; it is fine to use as a Parmigiano Reggiano or Pecorino Romano substitute in cooked food. Vegan suggestion: If cooking or using as a condiment, try using a blend of nutritional yeast, garlic powder, raw cashews and salt; my vegan peeps swear by this, and to me anything less processed is best.
NOTE: Parmigiano Reggiano uses rennet, which technically makes it non-vegetarian. American/domestic versions of this cheese called "Parmesan" are normally not made with rennet and can be used as a completely vegetarian substitute. These substitutes are good, but can be salty. I suggest using less or just reducing the salt in an other part of the recipe.

Ricotta: *Kite Hill* — I would use this in lasagna.

Mozzarella: *Daiya/Violife* 'Mozzarella Style Shreds' — it's perfectly melty for lasagna or added to a vegetable pasta or flatbread.

Cheddar / Provolone: *Violife* — slices melt better than shreds.

Cream Cheese and Butter: *Miyoko's* or *Kite Hill*

VEGAN BUTTER: I have tried a lot and I have read a lot. The general idea is "one size DOES NOT fit all." Unlike cow butter, plant-based butters can be wonderful, but different types and brands are best for different purposes. I don't generally cook with a lot of butter, but I do sometimes if I bake and sometimes to sauté certain things like grilled cheese, pancakes, etc.

My Choices:

Baking with Vegan Butter: I like *Earth Balance, Country Crock Plant Butter* (comes in sticks too)

Sautéing with Vegan Butter: *Miyoko's Creamery European Style Cultured Vegan Butter* is convincing and tasty

Definitely try some different brands for yourself as well. I do still use cow butter, so I do not spend a lot of time trying different vegan options; I know what I need it for and once I find it I am ready to roll. But if you like to use butter on bread alone, I suggest you do some homework, because many do not mimic butter well enough (in my opinion) for that use.

OTHER DAIRY:

Eggs: *Red Mill Egg Replacer* — I have used many different brands but I like Red Mill best. It's easy to use and, quite honestly, I find it makes fried foods crunchier than using egg; I like it better for pancakes too. I have had some issues baking, and usually use more replacer than the number of eggs called for in the recipe. *Energ-y* has also come highly recommended. I have learned to use baking soda and lemon as a frothy, binding egg substitute for certain recipes, particularly pancakes for which it works perfectly!

Milk and Yogurt: *Kite Hill* yogurts are our fave, Forager is great for all things cashew milk/yogurt, but my must for coffee and cereal is Califia Farms extra creamy almond milk. It just seems the creamiest to me, and I like that for coffee and mashed potatoes ☺

So, touring and traveling in Europe was particularly difficult in the early days because there were not a lot of vegetarians in Europe at the time, especially in places like Germany, or France or even Spain at the time. When we played in Germany, I remember Nina Hagen showed up to our show…at sound check, evidently she had heard that me and the singer, and the guitarist, Doug, were into Krishna Consciousness and were vegetarian. So she showed up with an entourage of Hare Krishnas and a huge feast prepared by them for us. It was really bizarre, sitting there having dinner with Nina Hagen and a bunch of Hare Krishnas. The show only got weirder and weirder as the night went on because this was Germany in the early '80s and the show wound up being full of Nazi Skinheads as well as the mostly Black, American Army guys who were hired to work security. It was an interesting show to say the least. — HF

the mains

the mains

FAST (30 minutes or less)

Riccioli (or Fusilli)
with Homemade Pesto and Broccolini

Pasta Primavera

Summer Squash and Basil Rigatoni

Curried Couscous

Pasta Puttanesca

Stuffed Peppers

Spaghetti alla Marinara

Cacio e Pepe

RICCIOLI (OR FUSILLI) WITH HOMEMADE PESTO & BROCCOLINI

SERVES 4

INGREDIENTS

16 ounces Rummo riccioli pasta (1 box) or alternatively DiCecco fusilli, though it is second place
2 cups 1-inch chopped broccolini, bottom dry bit of stem removed (broccoli can substitute as needed)
1–2 Tablespoons olive oil
Sea salt to taste

FOR THE PESTO

3 cups basil, chopped
½ cup pignolis (pine nuts), lightly toasted
2 medium cloves garlic (pressed in garlic press)
⅔ cup Parmigiano Reggiano
⅓ cup Pecorino or substitute
1 teaspoon fresh lemon juice
½ teaspoon superfine sugar or agave
½ cup good olive oil
fresh ground black pepper and salt to taste

I love pesto. Harley loves pesto. I have been making pesto for most of my adult life and have tried many delightful versions. But recently, for some reason, I happened to nail it so amazingly—like last night, and we couldn't understand why. *The back story* (as Harley says):

> When I was a kid, my mom had a huge framed poster in the kitchen with every kind of pasta known to humans. It had the name of each with a little picture, and I remember questioning the purpose of so many different shapes. My mother told me that the shape and size change the taste. *BULLSHIT*, I thought in my smart-ass child-brain. *But oh*, how wrong I was. Not all pasta is indeed equal, and that is true because of the ingredients, the process by which it is made and dried and, in fact, the shape.

What Harley and I learned last night is that pesto is its best self, *living its best pesto life*, when paired with Rummo brand (my fave) riccioli. OMG! Another level.

NOTE: this can be made vegan for sure, but I believe that great pesto depends on the greatness of the cheese. It's kind of like Cacio e Pepe—the cheese is the star of the dish. BUT please, if you want to make this vegan, do it—it will be delicious, I am certain. Try it with the nutritional yeast and a bit of cashew cream.

STEP 5

METHOD

1. Preheat the oven to 400°F.
2. Wash and trim and chop broccolini.
   Coat with light olive oil and add a little sea salt.
3. Place broccolini in a sheet or roasting pan; do not crowd pieces.
   Roast in the oven, tossing periodically, for about 15 minutes.
   You want them starting to brown but not burnt or too soft.
   Once cooked, set aside.
4. Wash the basil, pat dry *thoroughly* and pull off the leaves.
5. Add to Cuisinart or blender along with pignoli nuts and chopped garlic.
6. Pulse until coarsely ground.
   For a smooth pesto with little chunks of nuts and cheese, go directly from step 6 to 7.

Serve with stuffed artichokes and salad.

7. Drizzle in the olive oil. Add the lemon, sugar/agave, salt, pepper, and cheese or cheese substitute; drizzle the rest of the olive oil.
8. Cook the pasta per the box instructions.
9. Save some of the pasta water before draining it. Return the still-wet pasta back to the empty pot you boiled it in.
10. Add the pesto (as much as you like); mix to combine.
11. Toss in the roasted broccolini. A little of the reserved pasta water helps the sauce bind to the pasta.

*You can add more cheese if you like but it shouldn't need too much more.

FOR A CREAMIER PESTO, ALTERNATIVE TO STEP 7

7A Once the basil, nuts and garlic are ground, add and pulse in the cheeses, lemon juice, sugar/agave.

7B Then while the machine is running, slowly add in the olive oil.

PASTA PRIMAVERA

SERVES 4

INGREDIENTS

16 ounces Rummo or DiCecco Farfalle (bowtie) or orecchiette pasta (1 box)
4 Tablespoons extra virgin olive oil, divided
½ red onion, large 1-inch diced
2 small zucchini (cut in thin rounds)
2 cups fiddlehead ferns OR asparagus, cut into 1-inch pieces
1 cup sugar snap peas, OR 1 cup green beans cut into 1-inch pieces
6 medium garlic cloves, minced
½ cup Parmigiano Reggiano or substitute
3 Tablespoons chopped fresh Italian parsley
3 Tablespoons chopped fresh basil
salt and pepper, to taste

*2 Tablespoons cream or cashew cream (not necessary)

I was never a big fan of pasta primavera; I did not have much interest in pasta primavera growing up. I guess that is because red sauces, pesto and/or aglio e oglio (garlic, olive oil and some pasta water) were the house favorites. I always thought it was a "cream"-based dish and that was a no-no in my house.

I suppose I was exposed to risotto primavera first, and then the pasta version in Italy, and realized what I had been missing. This, of course, is deeply seasonally driven: the vegetables are the key to this elegant springtime dish.

NOTE: There are a bazillion primavera recipes out there—many are wonderful. You can mix and match the veggies you have. Just try to cut all your vegetables to be about the same size so they can cook evenly. If you're going to add vegetables of different densities, like winter squash and Brussels sprouts, you will want to start cooking the heavier items before adding the rest of the ingredients.

If you would like a creamier version, I offer my friend's cashew cream recipe below. Just add it along with the pasta water at the end.

NOTE: if you want this version, the cashews should be soaked overnight.**

**CASHEW CREAM

1 cup raw unsalted cashews
2½ cups water, divided
½ teaspoon salt

Soak the cashews overnight. If you forget to soak them, boil for about 10 minutes and then let them sit in the water for 30 minutes. Strain them and add to a high-speed blender or food processor with half the water and salt. Add more water if you want it creamier.

METHOD

1. Preheat the oven to 450°F.
2. Clean your vegetables and clip sugar snap peas as needed. Sometimes I cut the sugar snaps into smaller bites if they are big.
3. On a large heavy baking sheet, toss all of the vegetables with the olive oil, salt, pepper, garlic, and the chopped parsley and basil. Arrange the vegetables so there's not a lot of overlap.
4. Bake until the vegetables begin to brown, stirring after the first 10 minutes, about 20 minutes total. Be careful they don't overcook.
5. Meanwhile, cook the pasta per the box instructions in a large pot of boiling salted water until al dente. Drain, reserving ⅓ cup of the cooking liquid.
6. Toss the pasta with the roasted vegetables in a large bowl; add a bit of the reserved cooking liquid to moisten** (2 Tablespoons). Season the pasta with salt and pepper, as needed.
7. Add the Parmigiano Reggiano or substitute and serve immediately.

I would serve this with a mix of spring lettuces and herbs with a Dijon and shallot vinaigrette.

SUMMER SQUASH AND BASIL RIGATONI

SERVES 4

INGREDIENTS

¼ cup olive oil
4 cloves of fresh summer garlic, thinly sliced
1 small shallot, or small red onion, finely chopped
½ pound summer squash (zucchini, yellow straight neck squash, pattypan etc.), thinly sliced
ground salt and pepper
1 (16-ounce) box of DeCecco rigatoni
½ cup Parmigiano Reggiano and ½ cup Pecorino Romano (grated) or substitute
½ cup fresh basil leaves, cut in strips (I use a pair of scissors)
½ teaspoon crushed red pepper flakes
small squeeze lemon juice

This pasta dish is essentially just a big showcase for the exquisite freshness of the summer squash, that and the fresh basil and summer garlic. No need to make it more complicated than this. Those veggies need no help. This is a fast and simple summer meal.

NOTE ON GARLIC: You may find various varieties of garlic at your local farmers market—softneck, hardneck purple, elephant. Buy them all and experiment. You'll find there's great variety of flavor. Sometime between May and July you may start to see green garlic (easily confused with scallions/green onions). If you can find these, they would make a great addition to this dish. Just know that it is milder than traditional garlic, so you will want to add more in volume than the four cloves of garlic listed below. Whether you buy green garlic, or garlic that has already developed its papery skin, buy fresh whenever you can. Fresh garlic may be milder, but it is more flavorful. It kind of changes everything, in my opinion.

METHOD

1. Heat oil in a large skillet over medium heat. Cook shallot or onion until transparent.
2. Add garlic, stirring occasionally, until very lightly browned around the edges, about 4 minutes.
3. Add squash and increase heat to medium-high; season with salt. Cook, tossing occasionally, until squash begins to break down. Turn down heat once it begins sticking, and continue to cook until the squash is jammy and soft, 12–15 minutes.
4. Toss in crushed red pepper.
5. Meanwhile, cook pasta in a large pot of boiling salted water, stirring occasionally, until al dente. Save about ½ cup of the pasta water before draining it.
6. Transfer pasta to skillet with squash and add ¼ cup pasta water. Cook all together (on medium/low), adding most of the cheese in stages, along with more pasta cooking liquid only if needed. Cook until the sauce coats the pasta. Toss in lemon juice and most of the basil.
7. Portion pasta into bowls and add the rest of the cheese, basil, and any other pepper you might want, to taste (red or ground black).

I like to serve with a Caprese salad or a fennel salad.

CURRIED COUSCOUS

SERVES 4

INGREDIENTS

1¼ cups vegetable stock
1 cup uncooked couscous
1½ cups chopped broccolini or broccoli (florets and soft parts of the stem)
½ cup finely diced shallots (2 small)
¼ cup toasted pignolis
1½ Tablespoons apple cider vinegar
1½ Tablespoons olive oil
1 Tablespoon honey (I like eucalyptus, but try what you like)
1½ teaspoons mild Madras curry powder (more per your taste)
1 teaspoon turmeric powder
½ teaspoon red chile powder
½ teaspoon chopped green chile pepper (I use poblano or jalapeño)
1 teaspoon of minced fresh ginger
1½ cups garbanzo beans (chickpeas), preferably fresh and cooked, or canned
½ cup fresh feta (buy whole feta and crumble yourself) / or vegan feta substitute
ground salt and pepper to taste

I don't know where I first stumbled upon this recipe, but I have long since made it my own. This is one of those dishes I pull out every now and then, and Harley's reaction is always the same: "What is this? Is this Moroccan, but it tastes sort of Greek but sort of Indian," and he loves it every time. It does have some Moroccan, some Greek and some Indian elements, and they blend beautifully. Truly a spice-fusion dish.

METHOD

1. Cook the couscous per the package instructions, but with vegetable stock instead of water.
2. Toast pignolis in a dry skillet while the couscous is cooking. Keep an eye on them as they can burn very quickly.
3. Once both the pignolis and couscous are done, set them aside.
4. Chop the broccolini and steam so it is tender, but not mushy. We want it cooked, but crunchy.
5. Place the cooked couscous in a large mixing bowl with diced shallots, pignolis and cooked broccolini.
6. Mix the liquids together for the dressing: oil, vinegar, honey and the ginger in a separate bowl.
7. Add the dressing to the couscous and then all remaining ingredients, saving the feta last.

Mix very well. Taste for salt and pepper and serve warm.

*You can always add fried tofu (pages 29–30) to this dish for more protein.

Serve this with sautéed spinach and a Greek salad.

PASTA PUTTANESCA

SERVES 4–6

INGREDIENTS

If you eat fish — 4–8 anchovy fillets, depending on your taste. They will melt into the pan. Tamari sauce is a good vegetarian substitute for anchovies.

2 Tablespoons light olive oil

1 teaspoon crushed red pepper flakes

1 (16-ounce) box DiCecco spaghetti

4 cloves garlic, diced

1 (28-ounce) can of San Marzano or other good quality crushed tomatoes, undrained

½ cup pitted kalamata olives, diced

2 Tablespoons capers (in brine, not vinegar)

1 Tablespoon dried oregano

¼ cup chopped fresh Italian parsley

1 Tablespoon agave (to cut the acidity)

½ cup dry red wine (optional)

Salt and ground pepper, to taste

Harley likes heat! He's a spicy guy and loves food that's got some. But we both agree that heat for heat's sake is not the point. We like flavor, so the heat must allow for the flavors of the food to shine through. This recipe is my interpretation of what would be considered an "Arrabbiata" mixed with a Puttanesca, because one of the key flavors in Puttanesca is anchovy, which I have swapped out for a little more heat—alla Arrabbiata. So it's a *spicy prostitute* sauce LOL.

METHOD

1. In a large pot, boil your water and add a little salt and a few drops of olive oil.
2. In a large frying pan, add your olive oil, garlic, oregano, parsley, red pepper flakes, salt and pepper. Sauté for a few minutes on medium heat, moving everything around consistently.
3. If you use anchovies, add them now as well (and use a splatter guard because they will splatter).
4. After about 3 minutes, add your capers and olives and sauté for another 5 minutes, making sure nothing gets too brown; if things are going too fast just turn the heat down a bit.
5. Add the can of tomatoes and stir, stir, stir. I always place a splatter guard on the pan when I make sauce or else my entire stove is covered with tiny red splatters. I would add the wine now, if you choose to use it.
6. This mixture should cook down, with a lot of the liquid evaporating over about 15 minutes. Stir frequently and make sure the heat is not too high, so the ingredients are not sticking.
7. Your water should be boiling by now, so toss in the pasta and cook al dente.

Serve this with a simple salad and sautéed broccoli rabe.

STUFFED PEPPERS

SERVES 2

Stuffed peppers are an easy go-to winter main course. It has that minestrone-whatever-ya-got kind of quality and you can make them in so many different ways, with so many different ingredients. I guess I am kind of traditional, and I rely on the breadcrumbs...along with whatever else I feel like stuffing in there. I have seen peppers stuffed with quinoa, farro and rice; Sicilians use pine nuts and raisins. Play with this and make it your own.

INGREDIENTS

2 medium bell peppers
3 Tablespoons light olive oil
1 teaspoon crushed red pepper flakes
2 medium ripe tomatoes, diced
2 cloves garlic, diced
2 medium shallots, diced
1 Tablespoon dried oregano
1 Tablespoon chopped fresh Italian parsley
1 Tablespoon chopped fresh basil
1 teaspoon capers
1 teaspoon pitted chopped kalamata olives
salt and pepper to taste
1½ cups fresh plain breadcrumbs
1 Tablespoon crumbled feta
(use chunk feta and crumble it yourself)
— or substitute
* Instead of feta you can also use
Parmigiano Reggiano or nutritional
yeast/substitute

METHOD

1. Heat oven to 350°F.
2. Wash and halve your peppers. Pull out the innards, seeds, and stem. Rub inside and outer skin with a little bit of olive oil and a sprinkle of salt. Set aside on a baking pan.
3. In a frying pan heat the oil; add the shallots first and cook until they are translucent.
4. Add the garlic, pepper flakes, parsley, basil, oregano, and diced tomatoes. Add salt and pepper.
5. Move around on medium heat for about 3 minutes, then add the capers and olives. Continue stirring and mixing, bobbing and weaving, for another 5 minutes.
6. Add the breadcrumbs. Turn off the heat and mix in the breadcrumbs. The mixture should be thick and chunky and lovely ☺
7. Mix in the crumbled feta if you are using it.
8. Place your peppers open side up on a nonstick baking pan. Spoon in the breadcrumb mixture from the pan. They should be well-stuffed. Bake them in the oven until the top is browning.

Serve hot alongside a salad or minestrone soup or just some sautéed spinach.

SPAGHETTI ALLA MARINARA

SERVES 4

INGREDIENTS

1 (16-ounce) box DiCecco spaghetti or linguini if you prefer
1 (28-ounce) can chopped organic tomatoes with liquid—San Marzano if you can find
2 Tablespoons olive oil
2 cloves fresh garlic, minced
1 medium red onion, or 2 shallots, coarsely chopped
2 Tablespoons fresh Italian parsley, finely chopped
1 teaspoon fresh oregano, or ½ teaspoon dry
2 Tablespoons fresh basil, chopped
½ teaspoon red pepper flakes (optional)
1 squeeze (approx. 1 teaspoon) agave
salt and ground pepper, to taste
** sometimes I will add a splash of dry red wine*

Everybody has their own "marinara," right? It's the basic, the primary, the ground zero of Italian cooking in America. And like great pizza, it is fabulous for its simplicity and how great it tastes using the most basic ingredients. That said, like pizza, you can really fuck it up, and we have all had sauce that tasted like ketchup and pizza that tasted like cardboard.

My sauce is real simple. Like my favorite foods, it relies on the freshness of the ingredients. In the summer, I also make a variation of this with fresh tomatoes that I do not boil or roast first, and it has a light freshness to it that is lovely in warmer months.

METHOD

1. Heat a large pot of water to boil.
2. In a large frying pan heat the oil. Add onions first and let cook for about 3 minutes while you move them around.
3. Add garlic and do the same for another couple of minutes, and add salt and pepper (you want it to infuse the oil—that is why you add it now).
4. Add the parsley, oregano and basil.
5. Before anything gets too brown, add the tomatoes and start mixing well. Add the agave. As you are now mixing, please adjust for your own taste—more S&P, more basil, etc. You might also like to add the red pepper flakes for a touch of heat.

That's it. Let it cook for about 20–30 minutes, stirring regularly with a splatter guard. Once the pasta is cooked per box instructions, serve with grated Parmigiano Reggiano or substitute.

NOTE 1: Most people use sugar to "cut the acidity" of tomatoes, but I prefer agave. It dissolves quicker.

NOTE 2: This sauce should become your own, so please play with it as your taste buds prefer. There is no wrong way to do it—add capers or olives or whatever and enjoy!

Harley Flanagan:
"I know how you feel about vegetarian food [hate, deride, regularly talk shit about], but if you were gonna cook for a vegetarian, what would you make?"

Anthony Bourdain:
"A curry, definitely a curry. NO, wait… Cacio e Pepe."

CACIO E PEPE

SERVES 4

INGREDIENTS

2 cups grated Pecorino Romano, finely grated
½ cup Parmigiano Reggiano, finely grated
⅔ pound spaghetti (I like DiCecco)
2 Tablespoons extra virgin olive oil
2 Tablespoons ground black pepper
1 Tablespoon salt (for the water)
¾ cup pasta water

Another "peasant" dish gone Disney. With giant wheels of Parmigiano-Reggiano at every festival and street fair from New York to Tokyo to Venice, cacio e pepe is the gimmick food du jour, so very far from its humble beginnings in Lazio. But the simplest food is usually the best, and this one is no exception. Widespread use of Parmigiano Reggiano aside, the "authentic" version you will find in Rome is made with cacio, a sheep's milk cheese from Rome. It's hard to find in the States so I use Pecorino Romano AND Parmigiano Reggiano to satisfy my American palate. After all, recipes are so wonderful precisely because they really can't stay "authentic" for very long. Each cook brings her own style, his own palate, and their own culture to bear on the flavors of every dish. That is the magic. In the end, authenticity is what you make it.

Remember, cheese quality is key here, so I would not make this vegan and I would use authentic Italian cheese only.

METHOD

1. Bring water to a boil for the pasta, adding a few drops of oil and salt to the water. When the water is boiling, add the pasta and make sure to time it so you can remove it from the water about 2 minutes before done.
2. Pour the rest of the oil into a large frying pan. Leave the heat off.
3. Grind your pepper. Grate your cheese.
4. A few minutes before you strain the pasta, heat the oil on medium heat and add the pepper, moving it around, and cook until fragrant (about a minute). Add the pasta water and cook down on high until it is almost all evaporated. Turn off the heat.
5. Mix the cheese in a bowl with another ¼ cup pasta water. Mix well until creamy and then add to the pan with the pepper. Mix well.
6. The pasta will be ready now so drain it completely and add to the pan and mix, mix, mix. And serve immediately.

You can add a little more cheese on top when you serve, but it is not necessary.

the mains

STANDARD (30–45 MINUTES)

RISOTTO

I love risotto. Harley loves risotto. First of all, Arborio rice or carnaroli (if you can find it) is wonderful; the consistency of the kernels is so chewy and creamy, and it holds whatever flavors you add to it beautifully. It's a great rice. I have made it in so many ways. You'll find several delicious to enjoy. Enjoy them as they are, or use them as a template to create your own.

Risotto doesn't really take that much time to make, but it does require your love and devotion. You'll be paying attention and stirring for about 20 minutes straight. Other ingredients will require additional time to prepare. Know that with practice, this can become a reliable and simple staple in your repertoire. It's especially convenient as most of the ingredients are pantry items you can pull out whenever you like.

SAFFRON RISOTTO

SERVES 4

INGREDIENTS

8 cups vegetable stock
6–8 strands of saffron (a nice "pinch")
¼ cup olive oil
3 Tablespoons butter, or substitute
1 medium yellow onion or 2 shallots (I prefer shallots), finely chopped (about ½ cup)
2 cups Arborio or carnaroli rice
½ cup dry white wine (I've used Prosecco in a pinch and it works perfectly)
½ cup Parmigiano Reggiano or substitute

My version of the classic Risotto Milanese (a saffron risotto traditionally served with osso buco).

METHOD

1. Warm the broth on low heat, and keep warm and accessible throughout the risotto process.
2. Heat the oil and butter on low-medium heat, in a large-ish saucepan deep enough for the rice plus the liquid.
   Add the onion; sauté for about 2 minutes.
3. Add the saffron strands and continue to sauté for a couple of minutes; the color will just start to release from the strands, but shouldn't be more than 2 minutes.
   Season with salt and pepper.
4. Add the rice and coat well with the contents of the pan.
   Stir continuously for about a minute.
5. Add the white wine and stir until absorbed.
6. Lower the flame to low. In ½-cup increments start to add the veggie stock. Stir continuously so nothing sticks to the bottom of the pan.
   Keep adding broth approximately ½ cup at a time as the liquid is absorbed. The key is stirring—you are working with small doses of liquid, so it is easy for it to burn if unattended.
7. The rice should be firm but cooked al dente after about 15–20 minutes.
   Taste it to make sure.
   Then add the cheese. Stir continuously.
   Taste for any seasoning adjustments, salt, pepper, etc.

NOTE: Be careful with how much saffron you use. It seems like very little but saffron can be overpowering if you use too much.

Serve either risotto warm with some roasted asparagus and a butter lettuce salad.

PORCINI MUSHROOM RISOTTO

SERVES 4

INGREDIENTS

2 ounces dried porcini mushrooms
7 cups vegetable stock (approximate—you will check to see if more liquid is needed; see below)
½ cup water from soaked dried mushrooms
¼ cup olive oil
3 Tablespoons butter, or substitute
1 large clove garlic, finely diced
2 cups Arborio or carnaroli rice
½ cup dry white wine (I've used Prosecco in a pinch and it works perfectly)
½ cup Parmigiano Reggiano or substitute

I adore porcini risotto and make it frequently. The traditional version uses chicken stock, but having had both preparations, I think vegetable stock is perfect. In fact, when I've prepared a vegetable stock with plenty of mushroom stems, this is the perfect match.

METHOD

1. Soak the dried mushrooms in ½ cup lukewarm water for at least 20 minutes until rehydrated. Strain them through a cheesecloth or paper-towel-lined sieve and reserve the liquid.
2. Coarsely chop the rehydrated mushrooms a little (not too much). Set them aside.
3. Warm the broth on low heat and keep warm and accessible throughout the risotto process.
4. Heat the oil and butter on low-medium heat, in a large-ish saucepan deep enough for the rice plus the liquid. Add the garlic, sauté for about 2 minutes.
5. Add the porcini to the garlic; mix well. Season with salt and pepper.
6. Add the rice and stir continuously until the rice is well coated, about 1 minute.
7. Add the white wine and stir until absorbed; keep stirring.
8. Add the reserved mushroom soaking liquid and stir until absorbed.
9. Once the liquids are mostly absorbed you can start to add the veggie stock, ladling only enough in to coat the top of the rice each time.
10. Lower the flame to low. Stir continuously so nothing sticks to the bottom of the pan. Keep adding broth approximately ½ cup at a time as the liquid is absorbed. The key is stirring; you are working with small doses of liquid, so it is easy for it to burn if unattended.
11. The rice should be firm but cooked al dente after about 15–20 minutes. Taste it to make sure. Then add the cheese. Stir continuously. Taste for any seasoning adjustments, salt, pepper, etc.

ASPARAGUS AND WHITE TRUFFLE (OR WHITE TRUFFLE OIL) RISOTTO

SERVES 4

INGREDIENTS

1 pound fresh asparagus, ½-inch diameter
1 cup Arborio or carnaroli rice
2 cups vegetable stock
1 cup dry white wine
2 large cloves of garlic, big slices (so they can be removed)
1 shallot (small)
1 Tablespoon fresh Italian parsley (coarsely chopped)
⅓ cup Parmigiano Reggiano or substitute
4 Tablespoons olive oil
1 teaspoon white truffle oil
2 Tablespoons butter (optional) – substitute with oil if needed
ground salt and pepper, to taste

I love roasted asparagus and so does Harley. But the flavor is so strong and distinct when roasted that we prefer to keep it simple and eat it roasted as is. But steamed asparagus is another story. It is more delicate and blends in such a lovely way with the flavor of truffles. Early spring is the best time for asparagus.

Harley definitely tried truffles for the first time with me. I think we were at home and I made something with truffle oil. I had already known that he "hated mushrooms" and figured the similar earthiness of the truffle might be too mushroom-y for him, but I gave it a shot anyway.

I am certain he ate it before I told him what it was…it was one of those "what is this" moments we have had together many times. But he loved it before I described what truffles are and how they are harvested, though I think he liked the truffle pig concept and asked if we could maybe train our dogs to do something that useful ;) We are now **both** truffle-obsessed—black, white, and infused in oil, salt or honey… truffle it, and we will eat it.

METHOD

1. Clean, trim and steam or boil the asparagus. I like to use a 12-inch frying pan with a couple of inches of water and some sea salt. Make sure you do not overcook it—in fact, keep it on the crunchy side (in other words, only a few minutes, then quickly rinse in cold water so it doesn't keep cooking, because it will cook some more in the hot rice). Chop into 1" pieces and set aside.
2. Bring vegetable stock to a boil in a smallish saucepan (6–7"). Reduce heat to low or off and cover to keep warm.
3. Finely chop shallot and peel garlic cloves (if large, slice once in half).
4. Heat 3 Tablespoons light olive oil in another smallish saucepan (7") over medium heat. Add garlic and cook about 2 minutes until fragrant; discard the garlic.
5. Add the shallot and sauté until translucent.
6. Add chopped parsley. Season with salt and pepper.
7. Add the rice and coat with oil mixture. Cook until the rice begins to turn opaque.
8. Pour in ½ cup wine. Increase heat to medium-high and simmer until wine reduces, 3 to 5 minutes.
9. Pour ⅓ of the warm vegetable stock into the saucepan with the rice; cook and stir until absorbed.

10. In small amounts, pour in remaining stock, stirring constantly, adding more stock only once the last portion is absorbed. Continue stirring and cooking until risotto is tender and creamy, 15 to 18 minutes.
11. Remove risotto from the heat; add Parmigiano Reggiano. If using actual truffles, finely shave (with a truffle mandoline or vegetable peeler in a pinch) several shavings into the warm rice. If using truffle oil, drizzle 1 teaspoon of white truffle oil. Add the chopped asparagus and mix in well. Let stand for 3 to 5 minutes before serving. Add a touch more truffle oil if desired.

NOTE: cooking with real shaved white truffle (or black) is an art in which I am not well schooled. I eat it in Rome, where I think they do it best. I also love black truffles from Umbria—in every form. Truffle oil is a poor substitute, but it adds a lovely hint of flavor; be sure not to add it when the food is too hot as that neutralizes the aroma.

Serve warm with a butter lettuce salad and ricotta bruschetta.

ROASTED ROMANESCO RISOTTO

SERVES 4

INGREDIENTS

1 medium (approximately 1 pound) Romanesco
3 Tablespoons butter or light olive oil
1½ cups Arborio (or carnaroli) rice
1 medium shallot, finely chopped
½ cup dry white wine (optional)
½ cup Parmigiano Reggiano
4 cups vegetable broth
½ teaspoon sea salt (reduce if preferred)
½ teaspoon freshly ground black pepper

Romanesco is a type of broccoli/cauliflower. I first tried it in Italy and fell in love with the taste. But initially, I went gaga about its extremely wonderful *alien* good looks. First of all, it's chartreuse, which I realize is a pretty puke-y color, but I have always been obsessed with it…it attracts my inner alien. Then, of course, it is shaped like some sort of vegetable stalactite, which is mesmerizing in and of itself.

As is well described by consciouslykosher.com, "*The Romanesco's beauty is enhanced by its mathematically precise form: a fractal pattern and a Fibonacci sequence formed by the spirals of the buds. It is believed to have originated in Italy in the 16th century as a result of selective breeding.*"

All in all, for looks and taste, this is one of my all-time favorite vegetables. Don't fear it…it handles just like cauliflower or broccoli but keeps its wonderful density even better than its cruciferous cousins. It adds a unique, gentle flavor to any dish you would make with cauliflower or broccoli. BUT, if you can feature it, it is better to do so than burying it.

METHOD

The Romanesco

1. Heat the oven to 400°F.
2. Coat a large baking tray with light olive oil. Pull apart the Romanesco into smaller alien pods. Some pieces will be bigger, so I slice them in half or even in thirds. All in all, you want them a size that is not too large (no bigger than 1½ inches). Toss the pieces onto the tray, coating them with the olive oil. Add salt and pepper.
3. Roast for about 20–30 minutes, tossing every 10 minutes so they don't burn but become browned and their natural sugar releases. Once tender and browned, remove from oven and set aside.

The Rice

1. In a medium saucepan, heat the stock to a simmer and keep warm over low heat.
2. In a second large, heavy saucepan, melt 2 Tablespoons of butter or light olive oil over medium-high heat.
3. Add the shallots and cook until transparent but not brown. Add the rice and stir to coat well.
4. When the rice turns opaque, add the wine and simmer, stirring until the wine has almost completely absorbed, about 3 minutes.

5. Stirring frequently throughout this next process:
   Add ½ cup of the warm vegetable stock. When it is almost completely absorbed, add the next ½ cup and continue in the same manner—making sure the last addition is absorbed before adding the next—until the rice is tender to the bite and begins to look creamy, about 20 to 25 minutes.
   Before removing from the stove, stir in the roasted Romanesco.
6. Remove the pan from the heat. Stir in the Parmigiano Reggiano or substitute, pepper, and salt if needed. Serve immediately.

This dish is lovely with a simple arugula salad and roasted delicata squash.

ROASTED FENNEL RISOTTO

SERVES 4–6

INGREDIENTS

4 medium bulbs fresh fennel
1 Tablespoon butter or light olive oil
1 Tablespoon light olive oil
1½ cups Arborio or carnaroli rice
2 small shallots, finely chopped (about ⅓ cup)
½ cup dry white wine (optional)
¼ cup Parmigiano Reggiano and ¼ cup grated Gruyère or vegan substitute *vegan note: Parmesan substitutes are good but can be salty; use less or reduce salt in other parts of the recipe—for example, use low-sodium vegetable stock.
4 cups vegetable stock
1 Tablespoon chopped fresh Italian parsley
½ teaspoon sea salt (reduce if preferred)
½ teaspoon freshly ground black pepper

I love fennel. It was a staple in my grandparents' kitchen and my own. My grandfather loved it. While living in Italy I learned different ways to prepare it, as well, because as a child I had always eaten it raw. It is related to celery, but so much more complex. Yes, it has a bit of a licorice flavor, which can be surprising for people who do not cook with it, but once you do, I think you will fall in love.

METHOD

The Fennel

1. Preheat the oven to 400°F.
2. Lightly coat a large baking tray with light olive oil.
3. Cut the outside layer (or two if tough) and stalks off of the fennel and wash. Slice the bulb in half and then slice thin like you would an onion.
4. Slice 1½ shallots in the same way, reserving ½ a shallot for later.
5. Spread the sliced fennel and sliced shallots on the baking tray. Add a little salt and pepper and mix all together with your hands, then spread evenly across the tray.
6. Cook, mixing every 10 minutes or so, until the fennel and shallots are brown but not burnt; about 20–30 minutes.
7. Remove from oven and set aside to cool.

The Rice

1. In a medium saucepan, heat the stock to a simmer and keep warm over low heat.
2. Finely chop the reserved ½ shallot.
3. In a large, heavy saucepan, melt 1 Tablespoon of butter and 1 Tablespoon light olive oil over medium-high heat (or 2 Tablespoons olive oil if you are not using butter). Add the chopped shallot and cook until transparent but not brown.
4. Add the rice and stir to coat well. Cook and stir until the rice is opaque.
5. Add the wine and simmer, stirring until the wine has almost completely absorbed, about 3–4 minutes.
6. Begin adding the vegetable stock, ½ cup at a time allowing each addition to be absorbed, until the rice is tender to the bite and begins to look creamy, about 20 to 25 minutes.
7. Before removing from the stove, stir in the roasted fennel and shallot mixture.
8. Remove the pan from the heat. Stir in the Parmigiano Reggiano and Gruyère or substitute, chopped fresh Italian parsley, pepper and salt as needed. Serve immediately.

I serve this with a side of sautéed spinach and arugula salad.

VEGGIE BURRITOS

MAKES 4 BURRITOS

INGREDIENTS

4 large burrito-size tortillas
(I like gluten-free ones)
2 red, orange, or yellow bell peppers, sliced into ½-inch-wide strips
2 cups sweet cherry tomatoes, diced
1 medium red onion, chopped
1 medium clove garlic, crushed
2 cups vegan meat crumbles
2 Tablespoons chopped fresh cilantro
1 Tablespoon fresh Italian parsley
1 jalapeño or poblano chile, finely diced
1 (15-ounce) can black beans,
OR 2 cups cooked from scratch
½ cup shredded cheddar cheese or cheddar substitute
1 teaspoon lime juice
1 teaspoon Mexican (green) hot sauce
½ teaspoon chile powder
½ teaspoon crushed red pepper
½ teaspoon ground cumin
½ cup light olive oil
* If making this in the summer, try adding roasted corn cut from the cob and tossed in the mix

SPANISH RICE

1 cup long grain rice, or box of yellow rice (quicker) or package of Spanish rice (even quicker)
1 cup diced cherry tomatoes
1 cup vegetable stock
* if you use a boxed rice no need to add the spices below:
1 teaspoon chili powder
½ cup chopped fresh cilantro
1 Tablespoon cumin powder

We love Mexican food. And since the world has become so vegan-friendly, Mexican restaurants in NYC have so many more options for vegans and vegetarians. Once upon a time, Harley was left with a "veggie fajita" (peppers, onions and GAS) by default, but these days, everyone seems to come with creativity included. It doesn't take much. My rendition is just a bunch of flavors and textures we like, all happily wrapped up together.

[Many of these steps can be done simultaneously, i.e., prep tofu while roasting the peppers and while sautéing the crumbles, onion, garlic and tomatoes.]

***NOTE**: you can add tofu to this if you choose. But after making it several times I don't think it is necessary. If you use tofu, see tofu prep above, using salt, pepper and a little chili pepper blend. Once sautéed, brown and crunchy, set aside. OR use the tofu instead of the ground meat substitute.

METHOD

1. Drain and rinse the beans. Toss with chopped garlic, teaspoon chili powder, chopped cilantro and touch of olive oil and salt.
Set aside.

2. Heat oven to 400°F.
3. Coat the pepper strips in olive oil and a little garlic powder, chile powder, and touch of salt and black pepper;
roast until browning on all sides.
Toss occasionally for about 25–30 minutes.
Once cooked, set aside.
Lower oven temperature to 375°F.

4. **The rice**: Use a cup of yellow rice per the package cooking instructions or long-grain rice. Substitute vegetable stock for water. Add a cup of diced cherry tomatoes and spices above and cook per package instructions. Set aside when cooked (about 20 minutes).
4b: ***Alternatively***: If you are rushed, use a packaged brand of "Spanish rice." They are processed and freeze-dried and not as healthy as what you can make on your own, but when you are pressed for time, just do it.

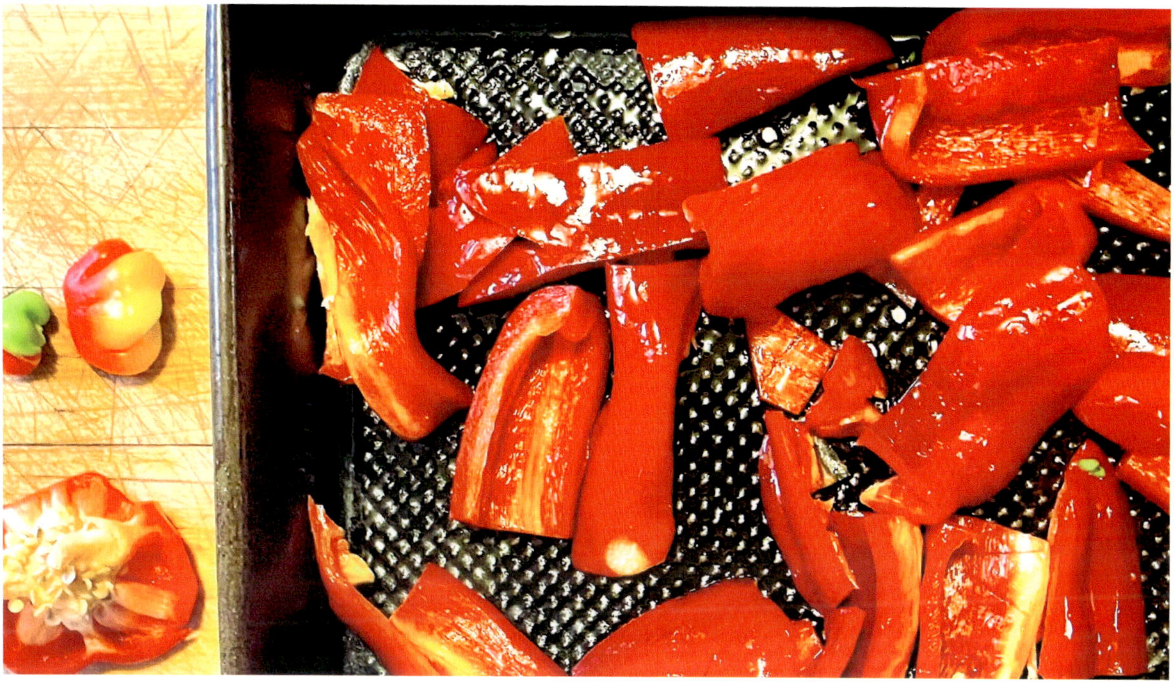

5. In a heavy frying pan on medium heat, add 2 Tablespoons of light olive oil.
6. Fry the onion first and then add the garlic, some chopped parsley and some chopped cilantro.
7. Add the vegan meat crumbles. Cook approximately 4 minutes, stirring occasionally.
8. Add the diced chiles, spices, salt and pepper and then the diced tomatoes; mix well as it cooks down. Taste it, it should taste good!

BURRITO ASSEMBLY

1. Take a tortilla and rub very lightly with olive oil.
2. Lay a wrapper on a flat clean surface. Add a couple of Tablespoons of rice; same for the sautéed vegan meat tomato mixture, some beans, sprinkle with cheese or its substitute, and a few roasted peppers. Don't put so much you can't fold it neatly. Fold burrito. I generally stick wet toothpicks in each before I put them in the oven, or flip over on the folded side to "seal" while cooking.
3. Bake on a lightly oiled baking pan for about 15–20 minutes; it should start to brown. Sprinkle with a little more cheese or cheese substitute on the outside; melt.

Pull those pups from the oven and throw a few red pepper flakes and some chopped cilantro on top. Yum.

I serve these with extra Spanish rice, black beans, and chips and guacamole.

TOFU SAGANAKI

SERVES 4

INGREDIENTS

1 block of firm organic tofu (dried and prepared as seen on pages 29–30)
3 cups cherry tomatoes, sliced in half
1 Tablespoon olive oil
3 Tablespoons vegetable oil (like peanut or canola)
4 scallions, white part only, chopped
2 cloves garlic, chopped
⅓ cup vegetable stock
2 Tablespoons ouzo or another unsweetened anise-flavored liqueur like sambuca (optional)
½ teaspoon chile powder
1 teaspoon chopped Italian parsley, plus more for garnish
1 Tablespoon chopped fresh oregano or 1 teaspoon dried oregano
salt and pepper to taste
2-ounce block feta, crumbled (buy the best block feta you can and avoid the pre-crumbled variety, it really makes a difference)

This dish is a bit of an improv: me riffing on a few recipes I like. As I understand it, in Greek, saganaki is simply fried cheese, the basis of which is called kefalotyri. The actual Greek dish I tried and loved was made with chicken and then I later had a variation made with shrimp. As unpleasant as cheese is with seafood generally, sort of like a Caesar salad this just works, maybe because I make mine with feta, which adds just the right acidic tanginess.

But with a vegetarian to cook for, I wanted to try to make this without any meat, so I used fried tofu instead and it was delicious.

METHOD

1. Heat the oven to 450°F.
2. Prepare the tofu, but instead of just dusting with salt and pepper, also sprinkle with red chili pepper powder and paprika.
3. Heat the vegetable oil in a nonstick pan until very hot. If you suck like me and never really know the temperature of the oil, just use the splash of water test. I take a tiny bit of water on my finger and throw it in the pan. If it essentially throws it back at me, the oil is ready for my tofu.
4. Set the tofu in the pan and it should sizzle a lot right away. Try one piece of tofu first to make sure it sizzles, and if not pull it out and wait a little longer. Tofu, unlike eggplant, is forgiving with frying.
5. Flip it as it browns and if your oil was the right temperature (sometimes I fail) the tofu should get really crispy on all sides. Once done, transfer to a paper-towel-lined plate to chill.
6. In a heavy baking dish (I prefer ceramic as I serve from the dish it's baked in), add halved tomatoes, chopped scallions.
7. Add the olive oil, chopped oregano and pepper, and very little salt as the feta is salty enough. Toss to combine.
8. Bake for 25–30 minutes, checking and flipping and moving it all around. As the liquid from the tomatoes starts to cook off, add small amounts of the vegetable broth to keep it all moist and mix it around.
9. Once the tomatoes and scallions are browned and tender, add the fried tofu to the pan along with the chunks of feta. Add the ouzo if using. Return to the oven to let it all cook down and the feta melt (about 10 minutes). You may decide to change the oven setting to broil at this point to get some dark brown on the feta—your call.
10. Sprinkle parsley on top and serve immediately with toasted French or sesame semolina bread to scoop up the sauce.

Serve with a Greek salad and roasted potatoes.

SPICY SESAME NOODLES WITH TOFU

SERVES 4

INGREDIENTS

1 pound dry lo mein noodles (I've tried with many different noodles; these hold the sauce the best)
1 cup English or Persian cucumbers, cut into matchsticks
1 carrot, shredded
3 cloves garlic, minced
½ cup fresh chopped scallions
1 package firm silken tofu (this is a very silky tofu that lends itself beautifully to this dish. The dish can be made with other types of tofu if you cannot find this one, but if you have the choice, choose this.)

SAUCE

1 Tablespoon creamy peanut butter
1 Tablespoon chunky peanut butter
¼ cup low-sodium soy sauce
1½ Tablespoons rice vinegar
4 Tablespoons toasted sesame oil (divided)
2 teaspoons mild honey or agave
1 Tablespoon minced fresh ginger
1 teaspoon chile powder
2 Tablespoons Sriracha (less if you like it less spicy, more if you want a little more kick)
Toasted sesame seeds (garnish at the end)

As a poor kid on NYC's Lower East Side, who became a vegetarian early on, Harley's food choices were limited to fries, pizza, bagels… and Chinese food (adapted to American taste, of course) was always the cheap go-to. Perhaps nothing is more Chinese-American than the ubiquitous cold sesame noodles. For Harley as a kid, it was cheap, filling, and delicious.

Harley and I both love cold sesame noodles with tofu, but making it the same silky and delicious way as our local Chinese restaurant eluded me for a long time—so I gave up, because why bother when I can order it and let Amy (the wonderful chef and owner of our local Chinese place), who knows better, take charge. Then came COVID-19 and the great quarantine which prompted me to complete this book and perfect every single recipe I could, in order to focus, be creative, and not lose my mind! Thanks to quarantine I make cold sesame noodles like a pro and Harley can have his childhood favorite whenever he wants. Silver linings are everywhere ;)

METHOD

1. Mix all sauce ingredients together and set aside. (Note: I add water to the mixture until it is the color of caramel and a bit thinner. I have found if it is thinner, it sticks better to the noodles and adds more flavor to everything.)
2. Cook the noodles per the package instructions until cooked but firm. Rinse under cool water to stop them from cooking. I then add a few drops of sesame oil and mix them in the colander to keep them from sticking together.
3. Transfer the noodles to a serving bowl. Add the chopped veggies and toss well. Mix the sauce well again and then pour into the bowl. Mix everything well so it is coated. I add tofu last and mix it gently, so it does not break.

Delish!!!

*I usually serve this together with vegetable fried rice and a butter or romaine lettuce salad with ginger/sesame dressing.

VEGETABLE THAI COCONUT CURRY

SERVES 4

INGREDIENTS

2 cups jasmine rice
1 Tablespoon peanut oil
2–3 Tablespoons Thai red curry paste (jarred or make your own if you can, it's easy—see opposite)
5 scallions, chopped white and light green parts—dark green keep to the side
3 garlic cloves, sliced thin
1 one-inch piece of fresh ginger, sliced thin
6 cups of sliced mixed summer vegetables (like zucchini, yellow squash, green beans, sugar snap peas, borlotti beans, sweet peas, Japanese eggplant, bell pepper, corn)
2 lemongrass stalks, bottom ⅓ only, smashed with a rolling pin or heavy pint glass (powdered lemongrass if you can't find fresh)
2½ cups vegetable stock
1 can (13.5 ounces) organic coconut milk
1 container firm organic tofu (cubed and pan-fried as described in the tofu prep above)
3 fresh basil leaves (large) or 6–7 little ones
1 Tablespoon vegetarian or vegan "fish" sauce. I use one made with mushrooms and seaweed.
1 lime wedge
salt to taste

Love, love, love the fact that we have a year-round farmers market just blocks from our house in Manhattan. And the summer months, with all the delicate squashes and insane tomatoes, are dreamy. The freshness of the vegetables, whatever season, always makes a big difference. Once I really started cooking like a vegetarian, I was amazed by the vast world of curries. They span so many cultures and cuisines and are all so rich and delicious. If/when you become a veg, you WILL make curry (Indian, Asian, West Indian)...it will happen, and it will make you and the people you cook for happy. This is definitely an Asian curry.

METHOD

For the Curry

1. Make the rice while you are preparing the rest. Rinse the rice in a strainer to remove excess starch. Add rice to a pot with 2½ cups water and ½ teaspoon salt. Bring the water to a boil, then lower to simmer, stirring occasionally. When done, let it rest. And then you will need to fluff it before serving.

Prepare your fried tofu and set aside on a paper towel.

2. Fry tofu as described on pages 29–30.
3. Heat oil in a large nonstick pan to low heat. Add 2 Tablespoons red curry paste and stir about 1 minute.
4. Add white and light green parts of the scallions, garlic and ginger. Stir constantly and do not let them brown, about 5 minutes.
5. Turn the heat to medium and add all the vegetables and the lemongrass. Cook and stir occasionally until the vegetables start to soften, about 10 minutes.
6. Add the vegetable stock and the coconut milk. Simmer for about 10 minutes until the vegetables are tender (not mushy).
7. Add the crunchy fried tofu and vegan or regular fish sauce and blend well.

Season with salt as desired, and for extra flavor add a touch more curry paste or vegan fish sauce until you are at your desired spice.

Serve with jasmine rice, top with chopped basil and dark green scallion slices and a lime wedge (optional). You can add a butter lettuce salad if you like.

THAI RED CURRY PASTE

INGREDIENTS

½ teaspoon ground coriander
1 teaspoon ground cumin
½ teaspoon ground black pepper
1 medium red bell pepper (seeds removed and chopped)
3 medium red chiles (Thai red chiles are best if you can find them)
1 stalk lemongrass (trimmed, then chopped; 1 teaspoon ground if you can't find fresh)
1 Tablespoon fresh ginger
3 cloves garlic, minced
1 small shallot or 2 green onions, finely chopped
1 Tablespoon ground turmeric
3 Tablespoons lemon juice
3 Tablespoons lime juice
6 scallions (chopped)
2-3 Tablespoons avocado, peanut or grape seed oil
1 Tablespoon maple syrup or honey
½ teaspoon sea salt (plus more, to taste)

Dump all ingredients in a food processor or a blender and blend!

*You can store in a jar in the fridge for about 2 weeks
or freeze it in the quantities you want to use.

MASSAMAN CURRY

SERVES 4

INGREDIENTS

1 (14-ounce) can coconut milk
½ cup vegetable stock
¼ cup homemade massaman curry paste** (or purchased)
½-inch piece fresh ginger, diced
1 large clove garlic, minced
1 large baking potato, diced into ½-inch to 1-inch cubes
2 cups fresh green beans, chopped in 1-inch pieces
1 small red bell pepper, diced
1 package extra firm tofu
1 Tablespoon vegetable oil (peanut)
4 scallions, sliced
¼ cup roasted peanuts, chopped

Massaman curry is one of our favorites. You can make the curry paste yourself if you are up for it. If you do, I promise it will be better than if you buy it ready-made; it always is. BUT if you can't, don't stress about it. Buy the massaman curry paste—this too will be delicious.

METHOD

1. Prepare the tofu (see pages 29–30) and set aside on a paper towel.
2. Heat oil in a saucepan on medium-high heat. Add ginger, garlic and curry paste and sauté for 30–45 seconds.
3. Add onions, pepper and potatoes and the coconut milk to the pan. Stir well.
4. Slowly add the vegetable stock as needed for a tender but not soft consistency.
5. When the curry starts bubbling, cover the pan and reduce the heat and simmer for 12–15 minutes, or until the potatoes are tender.
6. Add the green beans and cook for 2–5 minutes until cooked but still crunchy.
7. Add the tofu and simmer for another 2–5 minutes.

Let the curry sit for a few minutes. Sprinkle with chopped peanuts and serve.

Serve with jasmine rice, and a roasted vegetable.

****FOR THE MASSAMAN CURRY PASTE**

(makes a cup that can be kept for up to a month in the fridge)

12 dried chiles (or 2 Tablespoons crushed red pepper)
11 cloves garlic
3 lemongrass stalks or 3 Tablespoons dry lemongrass
1 medium shallot, thinly sliced
1½ pieces ginger, minced
1 Tablespoon vegetable oil (peanut if possible)
1 teaspoon ground cardamom pods
½ teaspoon ground cinnamon
1 teaspoon ground coriander
1 teaspoon ground cumin (I like Turkish)
½ teaspoon ground nutmeg
½ teaspoon ground turmeric
½ teaspoon coarse ground salt
½ teaspoon ground black pepper

You can grind all of this in a mortar and pestle or in a small spice grinder; just pulse it if you do so it is not too smooth. It should be a thick paste.

VEGETABLE LO MEIN

SERVES 4

Lo mein is another Chinese-American classic we love. It's one of those dishes where you can swap beef, chicken, shrimp, tofu—it doesn't matter because the flavor comes from the sauce and how it clings to the vegetables and noodles and protein.

INGREDIENTS

8-ounce package of lo mein noodles
1 Tablespoon light olive oil or peanut oil
2 cloves garlic, minced
2 cups fresh shiitake mushrooms, sliced (1 cup reconstituted if dry, drained)—shiitake are the best for this recipe with their unique flavor and meaty consistency, but you can also use oyster mushrooms or even sliced portobello in a pinch
1 red bell pepper, diced
1 carrot, diced
1 scallion, chopped
½ cup snow peas
3 cups baby bok choy, chopped in small pieces

SAUCE

2 Tablespoons low-sodium soy sauce (more if needed)
2 teaspoons mild honey
1 teaspoon toasted sesame oil
½ teaspoon ginger, ground
½ teaspoon Sriracha, more as preferred

METHOD

1. Make the sauce. In a small bowl, mix soy sauce, honey, sesame oil, ginger and Sriracha sauce. Set aside.
2. Cook noodles per package directions and drain. Add a few drops of sesame oil and mix noodles so they don't stick together while still warm. Set aside.
3. Heat the oil in a large pan or wok over medium heat.
4. Add garlic, mushrooms, bell pepper and carrot. Stir frequently until tender, about 5 minutes.
5. Stir in snow peas and bok choy. Cook for about 5 more minutes, stirring.
6. Once veggies are a tenderness and taste you like (still crunchy), add noodles, chopped scallions, sauce and toss.

Serve hot.

I make lo mein alongside fried rice or Szechuan eggplant and a salad.

ANGEL HAIR MUSHROOM "CARBONARA"

SERVES 4–6

INGREDIENTS

Pasta

1 (16-ounce) package of DiCecco angel hair No. 9 pasta
1½ cups fresh Italian parsley
1½ cups grated Parmigiano Reggiano or nutritional yeast
1½ cup grated smoked aged Gouda

Mushrooms

1 pound Hen of the Woods / maitake mushrooms
2½ pounds lion's mane / Pom Pom mushrooms
4 Tablespoons light olive oil
1 Tablespoon smoked paprika
¼ cup fresh garlic, finely diced
¼ cup light soy sauce
1½ Tablespoons maple syrup
salt and ground pepper, to taste

Cashew Cream

3 Tablespoons light olive oil
½ teaspoon red pepper flakes
1 large or 2 small shallots, diced
¼ teaspoon fresh garlic, finely minced
2½ cups raw cashews (soaked 10–12 hours or overnight)
¼ cup apple cider vinegar
½ cup white wine
½ cup water, as needed if the sauce becomes too thick (should be the consistency of a thin yogurt)
salt and ground pepper, to taste

There was a colorful cast of characters on my mom's side of the family when I was growing up. My "uncle" Bill Kresse was one of them: a very talented cartoonist for the *New York Daily News* his entire career, he was married to my "aunt"—really my second cousin Lorraine. He had a very robust moustache and beard, and I recall fondly that at Christmas he would let me take tiny Christmas ornaments and decorate his face. I think there is photographic evidence of this, and it is hysterical ☺

Uncle Bill introduced me to my first carbonara when I was very young, with my parents at one those vintage, right-outta-central-casting Italian places he loved in a remote part of Queens. According to him, what he introduced me to was "the best" he had ever had. They made it with angel hair pasta, and it was truly unforgettable.

Obviously the classic version of this dish relies heavily on the smoky-rich flavor of bacon or pancetta and the creamy complement of eggs and Parmigiano Reggiano. NOT vegan, or vegetarian-friendly. Harley is not a vegan, but he does not eat eggs, so while rethinking this dish I happened to stumble upon the sublime taste of roasted Hen of the Woods mushrooms…which absolutely tastes like super crunchy bacon. In fact, it is the most bacon-tasting non-bacon experience I have ever had. For this, I mix them with roasted lion's mane (or Pom Pom) mushrooms.

I know these mushrooms can be hard to find, but I implore you, go to Google and find them so you can make this dish. JUST DO IT—it's important.

NOTE: If these mushrooms are not an option this dish can be made with baby bellas or sliced portobellos; the smoked aged Gouda will make up for the smokiness.
The whole process will take about 1½ hours.

NOTE: Soak raw cashews 10–12 hours or overnight.
Sweat the lion's mane mushrooms per below.

METHOD

Stage 1

1. Heat oven to 400°F.
2. Thinly slice the lion's mane mushrooms and place on a paper towel and dust with salt. After about 15 minutes place paper towel on top and press out the water. Press a couple more times while you are prepping the other parts of the recipe; no need to add more salt.
3. Place a large pot of water on the stove turn on the heat. Add a touch of salt and oil to the water.
4. Separate the maitake mushrooms into small shreds, cut the dark hard bottom off (reserve for vegetable stock). Set the mushroom bits in a baking pan.
5. Drizzle the mushrooms with about 1 Tablespoon olive oil and with your hands coat the mushrooms. No need to wash them unless they are really dirty. Add salt and ground pepper, then spread them out.
6. Roast them on a low rack in the oven, so they are close to the heat underneath. They cook (and burn) fast so watch them and move them in the pan every 5–10 minutes. They will start browning and getting crunchy quickly.
   This should take about 20 minutes.

Stage 2 - Cashew Cream

1. While the maitake roast, make the cashew cream. Drain your cashews. You should be able to crumble them with your fingers.
2. In a frying pan, add 3 Tablespoons olive oil set on medium heat. Once hot, add red pepper flakes and let them sizzle. It shouldn't take more than a minute.
3. Add the onion and cashews and cook until they start to brown (about 15–20 minutes). Move the mixture around frequently.
4. Once caramelized add the garlic and white wine and simmer until half the liquid has cooked off. Then add the apple cider vinegar. Continue cooking for another 5 minutes. There should be very little liquid left in the pan. Let the mixture cool enough to put it in the blender or food processor.

Stage 3

1. By this time your maitake should be crispy and brown. Take them out and set aside on a paper towel until needed. Do not turn off the oven.
2. Remove the lion's mane slices from the paper towels and chop them up. Place in a mixing bowl.
3. Add the olive oil, garlic, paprika, soy sauce, maple syrup, salt and pepper. Toss well and spread them out in the baking pan you just used for the maitake mushrooms. Let them roast at the same 400°F for about 30+ minutes, moving them around every 15 minutes. My oven cooks fast so it took about 30 minutes to get them crunchy and browned.
4. The cream mixture should be cooled by now and ready to blend. You will need to add water as you go. You can make the sauce super creamy or a little chunky, which I prefer for this recipe. I like it to be granulated. Once blended to the consistency of your choice, return the mixture to the frying pan and add the cheese. Add some more pepper if you like and bring it to a quick bubble. Then turn the heat off. Taste it—it should taste amazing and smoky.
5. Take your lion's mane out of the oven; they should be crispy and brown. If they are not yet, wait to cook the pasta. Once they are cooked, then cook the pasta because it goes so fast.

6. Cook the pasta per the package instructions, noting that angel hair may take as little as 2 MINUTES. Scoop about 3 Tablespoons pasta liquid into the cream sauce.
7. Once your pasta is cooked al dente, drain it and return to the pot. Immediately stir in the sauce. You can decide how saucy or not you want the pasta. A thicker pasta can handle more sauce. Stir in the maitake mushrooms and the lion's mane mushrooms.

Sprinkle with fresh parsley and serve warm.

This is excellent accompanied by a simple arugula salad.

EUGENIA'S EGGPLANT PARM

SERVES 4–6

INGREDIENTS

1 large eggplant, sliced into 3⁄16" rounds (highly recommend a good mandoline to do this right)
3 cups of marinara sauce (see recipe page 43)
1 cup Parmigiano Reggiano or substitute, grated

*Mix of light olive oil and avocado or peanut oil for frying — ⅓ light olive oil to ⅔ one of the others

This is my grandmother Eugenia's recipe according to my mom. I was shocked and distraught (LOL) to learn that neither my grandmother nor my mother salt their eggplant prior to cooking. In Italy, from Luciana, I learned that this is a critical key to successful, non-mushy eggplant in whatever dish you make. My mother (and apparently my grandma) disagree. This recipe is so damn good. I am just doing what they tell me and throwing caution to the wind ☺

METHOD

1. Preheat oven to 350°F.
2. In a large frying pan, add oil to reach about ½-inch deep.
3. Test oil temperature by carefully dipping the handle of a wooden spoon into the oil. The oil is ready to fry if it bubbles steadily around the spoon. Place the eggplant slices in the oil; do not crowd them, and let them brown on both sides.
4. Once browned, remove with a slotted spoon or spatula and place on paper towels to drain.
5. Add a few spoons of sauce to a medium baking pan (about 9x12"). Arrange the slices with grated cheese and keep layering until all ingredients are done.
6. Bake for 30 minutes.

NOTE: My mom uses a very simple tomato sauce for hers. I prefer my marinara which is also very simple but adds a few more ingredients. You can use whatever tomato sauce makes you happy.

Serve hot with a salad or sautéed spinach or broccoli rabe.

STUFFED EGGPLANT

SERVES 4

Similar to stuffed peppers, a stuffed eggplant is kind of a free-for-all for me. You can really stuff it with whatever the hell you want, and I certainly have done so. This is a simple Sicilian variation, combining pine nuts and raisins.

INGREDIENTS

- 3 Italian eggplants (they are smaller than the regular ones and tend to be striped a lighter color purple) — about 8–10 inches and bulbous, unlike the long, thin Asian eggplant
- 3 Tablespoons light olive oil
- 1 medium red onion, diced
- 2 cloves garlic, minced
- ⅔ cup plain fresh breadcrumbs
- ½ cup raisins
- ¼ cup pignolis (pine nuts)
- ¼ cup Parmigiano Reggiano or substitute (less if you use nutritional yeast, it is saltier)
- ¼ cup fresh Italian parsley, chopped
- 2 Tablespoons fresh lemon juice
- Salt and ground pepper

METHOD

1. Preheat the oven to 350°F.
2. Halve the eggplants lengthwise and with a sharp small knife for precision (like a paring knife) run along the inside of the eggplants about ½". Then scoop the middle out and set aside. You want the shells to be about ½-inch thick. Sprinkle with salt and set flesh side down on a paper towel. Chop up the eggplant inside stuff.
3. Heat a medium frying pan and add 2 Tablespoons of olive oil. Add the onion, garlic, chopped parsley and chopped eggplant. Stir often for about 5 minutes. The onion should become translucent.
4. Turn off the heat and add the rest of the ingredients (breadcrumbs, pine nuts, raisins). Add a bit more salt and ground pepper to taste.
5. With a paper towel or clean dish towel, pat the inside of the eggplant shells dry, and place them skin-down on a nonstick baking pan. You can coat the shells with a little olive oil. Spoon the mixture from the pan into the shells. They should be well stuffed into little mounds. Rub the top with a little bit of oil and grind a bit more pepper on top.
6. Cover with tinfoil and bake for about 30 minutes. After 30 minutes, uncover and continue baking for 10 minutes more; they should get a little browned and crunchy on the top. At this point you can also add a little more cheese for the last 10 minutes.

Serve them hot with a salad or soup.

the mains

SLOW BUT WORTH IT (45 MINUTES–1 HOUR)

AND/OR ADVANCE PREP, LIKE MARINATING

TRADITIONAL FALAFEL

SERVES 4

1 HOUR TOTAL

INGREDIENTS

DO AHEAD: 1¾ cups dried chickpeas, soaked overnight in plenty of water

2 cloves garlic, crushed or use a garlic press
½ red onion, quartered
1 teaspoon ground coriander
1 Tablespoon ground cumin
½ teaspoon cayenne pepper or ground chile powder
½ cup chopped fresh cilantro
1 teaspoon salt
½ teaspoon ground black pepper
½ teaspoon baking soda
1 Tablespoon lemon juice
canola or peanut oil for frying

For dressing the falafel

2 Tablespoons tahini
2 cups chopped cherry tomatoes
Handful of arugula or other lettuce
Pita bread with pockets

Oddly, I went pretty much all my life without eating falafel, even though Mamoon's is one of the best places for falafel and it is a classic NYC staple. I feared the chickpea, but I have overcome my fear.

As far as dips and small plates and tapas are concerned, I love it all! I love Spanish and Greek and Turkish and Lebanese cuisine with all the little tastes and bites and dips with fabulous breads. I need nothing else, in fact. Harley does not agree; now that he is a foodie (though he will never admit to that) he needs more substance than just dips and small plates…but what does he know?!

Give me a glass of Barolo and this stuff and let's call it a (good) night ;)

METHOD

1. Set the oven to 200°F and put the pita inside to keep it warm.
2. Drain beans and dry them as much as possible. Transfer to a food processor or blender and add ingredients from the list, garlic through lemon juice.
3. Pulse until mealy but not puréed. Add a little water only if the mix seems too dry to hold together. Be careful; if it is too wet it will fall apart when cooking.
4. Taste the mix for any more seasoning (lemon, salt, pepper, etc.).
5. Add 3 inches of oil to a deep saucepan. For frying I generally use a little pan, so I don't need as much oil, and only cook 4 balls at a time. Turn stove to medium-high and heat oil to about 350°F or until a drop of batter sizzles fast and intensely.
6. Scoop a big Tablespoon of mixture into your hand and shape into a ball. I like them the size of smallish ping pong balls and then I flatten them a little. I make about 4 and set on a plate.
7. Place the slightly smooshed balls into the oil. They should drop and then float to the top sizzling like crazy. And if your oil is good and hot, they will brown quickly, so move them around with a slotted wood spoon or similar.
8. While the 4 are frying I make the next batch and have them ready to drop in.

Back in the '80s there were really only a couple of vegetarian restaurants on the Lower East Side; Ahimsa was one of them, and they also had a health food store. There was Vegetarian Paradise and House of Vegetarian in Chinatown…and that was about it. Before that the only place that I could go for purely vegetarian food was either the Hare Krishna temple or the Seventh-Day Adventists because they are also vegetarians. So, when I was living in the squats as a kid, I would go to where they were serving food in the park and that was pretty much how I would survive, between the Seventh-Day Adventists, the Hare Krishnas, and shoplifting, and the cook at Ahimsa who used to sneak me and my band members food every day. And he passed that tradition on to the employees that replaced him. And I believe that they still feed some of my old band members to this day. — HF

Fry in batches but do not crowd them (they should not touch). They should be dark brown and very crunchy on the outside.

I pull them out with a frying basket or slotted spoon and set them on a paper towel while I fry the rest until I serve them.

9. Take a warm pita from the oven. Open it and spread some tahini on the inside. Stuff a little arugula and lightly salted sliced tomatoes (just a couple of sliced cherry tomatoes is enough). Hopefully you have enough room for a couple of falafel balls. I tend to cut them in half and try to distribute the 4 halves evenly in the pita.

Harley adds raita to his sandwich; I do not disagree with that choice! There are no rules anymore about what to serve with what. The world is all fusion all the time and that's awesome because so many cultural flavors blend beautifully together.

I like to serve falafel with cucumber raita (page 146), dal (page 92), baba ghanoush (page 147) and naan bread or pita.

VEGETABLE LASAGNA

SERVES 4–6

2 HOURS TOTAL

This recipe is a mélange of different knowledge. My mom and grandparents made a traditional meat lasagna (Italian sausage and Bolognese sauce). I took a few elements that I learned living in northern Italy and modified it all *for the Hardcore Vegetarians in my life.* There are several steps, but it is worth it. And if you make it in a generous-sized pan, you can freeze the leftovers and then not have to think at all the next time you want it!

INGREDIENTS

1 large eggplant
3 zucchini
1 (28-ounce) can organic crushed tomatoes
1 medium red onion, finely chopped
2 medium cloves garlic, minced
2 Tablespoons fresh Italian parsley, finely chopped
2 Tablespoons fresh basil, finely chopped
1 teaspoon fresh or ½ teaspoon dried oregano
1 teaspoon fine sugar or agave
1 cup meat substitute, protein "grilled" crumbles (Gardein is my favorite)
2 Tablespoons olive oil
2 cups peanut oil or other oil for frying
2 cups fresh ricotta (or substitute)
2 cups fresh mozzarella (or substitute)
1½ cups Parmigiano Reggiano (or substitute)
1 package DiCecco lasagna noodles
2 eggs or egg substitute and a dash of milk
½ teaspoon freshly ground black pepper
salt to taste

1 large and deep baking pan

NOTE ON LASAGNA PASTA: The pasta you have to boil first works better. They make pasta that you can just put in the oven "hard" and it will cook with the other ingredients, but it does not cook as evenly. Your choice; I do either, depending on how lazy I feel.

METHOD

First Steps

Most of these can be done at the same time, so do that or it will take FOREVER.

1. Slice the eggplant into ½-inch slices (skin on). Lay them on a flat surface and lightly salt. Let them sit for 20 minutes until they start to sweat. Pat dry, flip and repeat on side two. Pat them dry and set aside.

While eggplant is sweating…

Preheat oven to 400°F if doing the zucchini step in order.

Make the Sauce

2. In a medium-heavy saucepan heat 1 Tablespoon olive oil and sauté onion until transparent, not brown; add minced garlic, chopped parsley, basil and oregano and cook, moving around for about a minute until fragrant.
3. Add the grilled "crumbles" and then pepper and a little salt.
4. Sauté until browned and then add the crushed tomato. Stir well and let simmer for 10 minutes.
5. Add the sugar or agave. Allow the sauce to bubble a little but not boil for a good 20 minutes, and stir now and then.
6. Remove from heat and set aside.

Cook the Pasta

Cook the pasta per the box instructions. Once cooked, I leave the noodles in the colander and add a little olive oil to keep them separate from each other while they wait to be assembled into the lasagna.

Roast the Zucchini

1. Slice the zucchini lengthwise (¼-inch). Coat with olive oil and a little salt.
2. Lay on a baking tray next to each other and bake in the 400°F oven. Brown on each side (about 10–15 minutes per side).
3. Once cooked, set aside.

NOTE: Reduce oven temperature to 375°F.

Fry the Eggplant

1. In one bowl mix the eggs (or egg substitute) with the milk.
   In another bowl add plain breadcrumbs and salt and pepper.

I also add a little grated cheese or cheese substitute to the breadcrumbs.

2. Take your plate of sliced eggplant and set next to the bowls. Dip one slice at a time in the egg, remove excess egg, and then coat in breadcrumbs and set aside on a plate for frying.
3. Heat the ½ cup or about 1 inch depending on the depth of the pan, peanut oil in a heavy nonstick pan.

***NOTE ON FRYING**: *It needs to be between 350°F and 375°F. If you don't have a thermometer, you can test the temperature by gently placing the end of a wooden spoon in the oil. If bubbles form around it, your oil is ready. Alternatively, if you have an air fryer, "fry" at 375°F for 12 to 14 minutes, flipping halfway through.*

4. Place your coated eggplant slices in the pan, be sure to not crowd them—they should not touch. Brown each side.
5. Remove each slice when fully browned. Place on paper towel waiting to assemble into the lasagna.

Final Step

NOW—you should have your pasta, your sauce, your veggies and cheese or cheese substitutes. You are ready to assemble the beast!

1. Rub a little olive oil on the bottom of the baking pan.
2. Lay a single first layer of the cooked pasta along the bottom. Some overlap is good.
3. Then add a thin layer of sauce.
4. I start with some strips of the roasted zucchini along with about 6 Tablespoons of ricotta or ricotta substitute. Sprinkle this layer with a little grated Parmigiano Reggiano or substitute.
5. Lay the next layer of pasta down. Press gently to make even.
6. Add another layer of sauce.
7. Lay the slices of eggplant evenly and then scatter chunks of the fresh mozzarella or substitute with another sprinkle of grated Parmigiano Reggiano or substitute.
8. Repeat these layers until you have used all your ingredients, and the last layer, I like to make just sauce and grated cheese.
9. Cover with one last layer of pasta and coat with a thin layer of olive oil.

I like to take a very sharp knife and cut it into portions before I cook it—my mommy taught me that and it really helps extract the portions once cooked.

10. Cover the pan with tinfoil (do not touch the pasta with the foil). Bake for 25–30 minutes.

Once cooked, take the pan out of the oven, and let it rest covered for 10 minutes, then take the foil off and serve. You can take the foil off and return to the oven broiler for a few minutes, if you want the top to brown a bit; I go either way.

I serve lasagna with a simple salad—that's all you need, besides a glass of Barolo ;)

LIME TOFU

SERVES 4

40 MINUTES COOK, PLUS 3 HOURS FOR MARINADE

INGREDIENTS

Marinade

1 package organic firm tofu
3 Tablespoons soy sauce
1 lime (juice of)
1 clove garlic, minced
1 teaspoon turmeric powder
1 teaspoon mild Madras curry powder
¼ cup vegetable stock

1¼ cups white wine
2½ Tablespoons lime juice
1 small carrot, finely sliced
½ leek, white and light green portion only, finely sliced
5 scallions, finely sliced
1 Tablespoon of crushed ginger
1¾ cups vegetable stock
1 teaspoon corn flour
½ teaspoon sugar or agave
1 teaspoon soy sauce or tamari
2 limes

This one takes a little work, but it is a delicate beauty worth the effort.

METHOD

1. Cut the tofu into 1-inch cubes and place in an airtight container with the marinade ingredients. Let the tofu marinate for at least 3 hours. Rotate the container every so often to make sure the pieces are well coated.
2. Boil the white wine and lime juice until reduced to about ¾ cup and set aside.
3. Take the tofu out of the marinade and drain so it's dry. Save the marinade.
4. Heat the peanut oil and sear the tofu on both sides, flipping when each side is brown. Remove from the pan and set aside.
5. Sauté the carrots, ginger and leeks in that same pan, then add the reduced wine and lime, the marinade and the rest of the vegetable stock. Simmer until the vegetables are tender.
6. Using the corn flour and about 2 Tablespoons of water, mix into a slurry. Add the corn flour to thicken, add the tofu, sprinkle with spring onions/scallions, add sugar/agave and soy sauce to taste.

ALOO GOBI

SERVES 4

1 HOUR TOTAL

INGREDIENTS

2 medium yellow potatoes, cubed (about 2 cups)
1 small cauliflower, chopped into small florets (about 2 cups)
3–4 teaspoons coconut oil
½ teaspoon cumin seeds
1 medium yellow onion, medium chopped
¾ teaspoon ginger paste
¾ teaspoon garlic paste
2 medium tomatoes, chopped (about ½ cup)
½ teaspoon turmeric powder
¼ teaspoon chile powder
1 teaspoon coriander powder
¼ teaspoon garam masala
2 Tablespoons chopped fresh cilantro
Salt to taste

Aloo gobi is one of our faves and we regularly order it from the Indian places we frequent. Having tried so many, I thought, *how hard could it be?* So, I made my own version and it was delicious.

METHOD

1. Parboil the cauliflower and potatoes separately in salted water (3–5 minutes for the cauliflower, 15 minutes for the potatoes). Set aside.
2. Heat 2 teaspoons coconut oil in a pan on medium heat. Add cauliflower for 2–3 minutes, stirring, then add the potatoes. Once they start to brown on all sides, pull them out and set aside once again.
3. In the same pan add another 1½ teaspoons of oil and add cumin seeds cooking until they start to crackle. Then add the chopped onion, and sauté until translucent, about 2–3 minutes. Add the garlic and ginger pastes and cook for another 2–3 minutes, mixing. For a thinner consistency, feel free to add a couple of Tablespoons of water and cook a couple of minutes longer as needed.
4. Add the chopped tomatoes and stir until they start to break down, another 3–4 minutes.
5. Add turmeric, red chile powder and coriander. Mix all well. Let this all cook for 2–3 minutes.
6. Then add the potatoes and cauliflower back into the pan. Add the garam masala and cook on low heat for 5–6 minutes, stirring well.
7. Add salt and cook another 5 minutes. If the mixture is getting dry or sticking, I add a Tablespoon of vegetable stock (or water).

Sprinkle with chopped cilantro and serve with basmati rice, raita and naan.

SOBA NOODLES WITH MISO GLAZED TOFU

SERVES 4

1 HOUR TOTAL INCLUDES TOFU PREP

INGREDIENTS

1 Tablespoon + 1½ teaspoons peanut oil, divided

1 (14-ounce) package firm or extra firm tofu

Sauce

1 Tablespoon peanut oil

3 Tablespoons rice vinegar

2 Tablespoons white miso

1 Tablespoon minced ginger

1 Tablespoon minced garlic

1 Tablespoon soy sauce

1½ teaspoons honey

1 teaspoon toasted sesame oil

I love this recipe. It is THE go-to when I have no idea what to make for dinner. It never disappoints. The tofu is so sublimely sweet and spicy and glazed to perfection and with a bit of crunch, it is unstoppable. Unstoppable tofu!

METHOD

1. About 1 hour before making this, prepare your tofu. Drain, slice down the middle and wrap in paper towel or a clean dishtowel to absorb the water.
2. Combine all the sauce ingredients in a bowl and mix well. You will likely have to work the miso into the rest of the ingredients, but the soy and vinegar will soon break it down, so it is smooth and integrated. I work it in with the back of a spoon. Once it is all smooth set aside.
3. Cook the noodles per package instructions with a little oil in the water; drain and cool with cold water. Pour the noodles into a second mixing bowl and add ¼ cup of the miso mixture and stir together well so noodles are coated. Set them aside.
4. Slice tofu into 1-inch pieces.

Soba and assembly

4 ounces soba noodles or lo mein noodles
2 cups thinly sliced fresh shiitake mushrooms
3 cups asparagus in 1-inch pieces OR 3 cups sliced thin baby bok choy (I like this recipe both ways)
¼ cup sliced scallions

5. Heat a large nonstick pan on medium, add 1 Tablespoon peanut oil and coat the bottom. When the pan sizzles if you flick a drop of water in it, add your tofu. It should sizzle right away, so do one piece at a time to make sure the oil is hot enough. Sauté for about 5 minutes per side, but make sure you have a nice golden-brown color before you flip.

6. Once both sides are golden, add 1 Tablespoon of miso mixture to the pan. It will splatter and sizzle. Quickly toss the tofu so it is coated and move it around so all sides brown with the miso mixture evenly. Once they are coated and caramelized, turn off the heat and set the tofu aside in a bowl.
7. Heat the same pan again, add the remaining oil, toss in the mushrooms and veggies and sauté until tender (mushrooms get a bit crispy too)—about 5–8 minutes, moving around as they cook.
8. Add the remaining miso mixture and coat the veggies; cook an additional couple of minutes.
9. Toss the noodles into the veggie pan and mix, then transfer to a serving bowl. Top with the tofu and sprinkle with the scallions. SO GOOD!

I generally serve with Szechuan eggplant and fried rice.

SZECHUAN EGGPLANT

SERVES 4

30 MINUTES, PLUS 30 MINUTES TO 1 HOUR BRINING TIME

INGREDIENTS

- 1½ pounds Japanese eggplant (4×10-inch-long purple beauties), cut into ½-inch half-moons
- 2 teaspoons salt
- 2 Tablespoons organic corn starch
- 4 Tablespoons peanut oil
- 4 cloves garlic, minced
- 2 teaspoons fresh ginger, finely minced (divided - 1 teaspoon for sauce)
- 5-10 dried chiles
- 2 scallions, chopped for garnish

STEP 1

Sauce

- 1 teaspoon ground black pepper
- ¼ cup low-sodium soy sauce
- ½ teaspoon red pepper flakes
- 1 teaspoon minced garlic
- 1 teaspoon minced ginger (see above)
- 1 Tablespoon toasted sesame oil
- 1 Tablespoon seasoned rice vinegar
- 1 Tablespoon mirin
- 3 Tablespoons mild honey
- ½ teaspoon Chinese 5-spice

This recipe is insane. I played with the flavors a bit based on what I had available, and the result, well—it made me feel like a professional chef. No joke—this is so seriously tasty, and professional-looking…we were both blown away.

NOTE: Full transparency, I have failed at making this several times. When I say fail, usually frying is involved and invariably means my oil was not hot enough so my eggplant soaked it up like a sponge. DON'T LET THIS HAPPEN TO YOU. Fry at the right temperature.

P.S. Harley is not a big fan of eggplant other than "parm," so at some point I made the incredible sauce for this dish, then sautéed sugar snap peas and let them cook down in the sauce. And WOW, that was pretty amazing as well. Just a little FYI. Don't hesitate to play with this one.

METHOD

1. Place eggplant in a big bowl of water with the 2 teaspoons of salt, brining the eggplant. Make sure the pieces are submerged. Let them soak for at least ½ to 1 hour. Then pour out the water.
2. Combine all the sauce ingredients in a small bowl. Set aside.
3. Pat the eggplant pieces dry with a paper towel, making sure the pieces are completely dry. Toss the eggplant with the corn starch and make sure the pieces are coated. Work in batches to fry, and this is key because they do not cook well and will get soggy if you crowd them.
4. Add 2–3 Tablespoons oil to a medium frying pan or wok and heat the oil until it is very hot, but not smoking. Set the first batch in the pan, but don't rush to toss it. Let one side get golden brown (about 7 minutes), then flip the pieces with tongs to brown the other side for another 7 minutes. Set the first batch aside on a paper towel and cook the second batch.
5. Once all the eggplant is cooked and set aside, add 1 more Tablespoon of oil to the pan at medium heat and add 1 teaspoon ginger to the pan—this WILL splatter so turn on the fan and/or use a splatter guard.
6. Add the dried chilies and stir for a minute or so.
7. Pour the sauce into the pan and let it simmer for about 20 seconds, then while it's bubbling, add the eggplant back into the pan and toss gently for about 1 minute.

Serve hot with the chopped scallion garnish.

I like to serve this with soba noodles with miso glazed tofu or vegetable fried rice made with black rice (because it's so pretty) or jasmine rice, OR a butter lettuce salad with sesame ginger dressing.

INDIAN VEGETABLE CURRY

SERVES 4–6

INGREDIENTS

2 cups cauliflower florets
1 cup peas (frozen are fine)
1 carrot, diced
2 cups green beans, chopped to 1-inch pieces
1 zucchini or winter squash (like delicata) cut into small cubes, about a cup
3 medium yellow potatoes, 1-inch cubed
6 medium tomatoes (canned whole are fine)
½-inch fresh ginger, minced
1 green chile (leave seeds in for heat), diced
2 Tablespoons vegetable oil or coconut oil
¼ cup vegetable stock
½ teaspoon cumin seeds
⅛ teaspoon asafoetida powder
¼ teaspoon turmeric powder
¼ teaspoon ground red pepper
1 Tablespoon coriander powder
1 teaspoon sugar
1 teaspoon sea salt
1 Tablespoon corn starch
½ teaspoon garam masala

2 Tablespoons chopped fresh cilantro

As you now know, we eat a lot of curry in our house: Indian, Thai, Vietnamese, Malaysian, Chinese…there is nothing that can't be curried. But in the winter when root vegetables are abundant, I tend to gravitate toward a rich Indian curry that works so well with hearty vegetables; it is substantial, spicy and satisfying.

METHOD

1. Mix corn starch with ¼ cup of water and set aside (mix every once in a while, or it becomes concrete).
2. Boil water in a medium saucepan and parboil the potatoes, carrot and cauliflower florets for about 5 minutes. Don't overcook. Set aside hot.
3. In a blender or Cuisinart, blend 5 of the tomatoes, the green chile and ginger into a chunky purée.
4. Slice the last tomato lengthwise and set aside.
5. In a heavy saucepan, heat the oil. Test the heat by dropping a cumin seed in it—if it splatters, add all the cumin seeds and asafoetida.
6. As the seeds pop, add in the tomato mixture, coriander, turmeric, sugar, and salt. Cover and cook over medium heat for about 5 minutes. The mixture should be chunky and not watery.
7. Add the potatoes, cauliflower, and carrot and ¼ cup vegetable broth. Cook covered for another 5 minutes.
8. Add the green beans, zucchini, peas and cook all together for another 10 minutes uncovered. We want firm, not mushy vegetables, so watch them as they cook.
9. Add the corn starch mixture to thicken and stir in well. Add a little more vegetable broth if needed for the consistency you prefer, more broth if you want it less chunky.
10. Turn off the stove, add the sliced tomato, garam masala and chopped cilantro. Stir well and cover for a few minutes before serving.

I serve this with basmati rice and/or naan and a butter lettuce salad.

SAVORY WILD MUSHROOM BREAD PUDDING

SERVES 6

2 HOURS TOTAL

We have become mushroom-crazed. Wild mushrooms are so healthy and delicious, and the more you learn about them, the more magical (literally) they become. And besides the truly "magical" psilocybin mushrooms, the natural health benefits of wild mushrooms are endless. From immune support to anti-inflammation to cognitive support and focus, the vitamins and minerals they supply are endless: fiber, B, A, folic acid; they may also mitigate the risk of developing conditions like Alzheimer's, heart disease, cancer, and diabetes. WTF!
If you aren't eating them, start.

INGREDIENTS

- ½ pound loaf day-old sourdough bread or focaccia, cubed
- 2 Tablespoons butter (or vegan butter), divided
- 2 Tablespoons olive oil, divided
- 1 cup (approximately 3 small) leeks, chopped (white and light green parts only)
- 2 cloves garlic, minced
- ½ pound oyster mushrooms, coarsely chopped
- ½ pound cremini mushrooms, coarsely chopped
- 1½ cups creamy almond milk, or whole milk
- 4 eggs, or egg substitute
- ½ cup Parmigiano Reggiano, or substitute, grated
- ½ cup Gruyère cheese, or cheddar substitute (I have not found a Gruyère substitute), shredded
- 1 teaspoon dried thyme
- 1 teaspoon fresh Italian parsley
- salt and ground pepper, to taste

METHOD

1. Grease a heavy baking/casserole dish (about 5 quarts) with 1 Tablespoon olive oil. I would use an attractive dish as you will serve from the baking dish, and we like aesthetics ☺
   Add the cubed sourdough.
2. In a frying pan, melt half the butter with the rest of the olive oil, and sauté the leeks on low heat for about 8–10 minutes with salt and pepper.
3. Add the garlic and cook for about 2 minutes more, then add the chopped mushrooms and herbs and continue to sauté for another 10 minutes until well blended and starting to brown.
4. Spoon the mixture over the bread in the baking dish.
   In a separate bowl mix the milk, eggs, and ⅔ of the cheese together. Pour this mixture into the baking dish. Let this stand covered for 30 minutes.
5. Preheat oven to 375°F.
6. Uncover the baking dish after 30 minutes and sprinkle the remaining cheese on top. Place in the oven and bake for about 45 minutes or until the top is brown and crunchy. Take a look after 30 minutes to see where you are. My oven runs hot, so sometimes I have to turn things down so they do not burn. It should be bubbly and browning with crunchy edges when it is done.

Serve hot with a simple salad, and sautéed broccoli rabe which has a nice bitterness to counter the richness of this dish.

PUMPKIN LASAGNA

SERVES 4–6

INGREDIENTS

Pumpkin Sauce

1¾ cups pumpkin purée (15-ounce can)
1 cup heavy cream or vegan substitute
⅛ teaspoon of each pepper, sage, cinnamon, powdered ginger, nutmeg, allspice
½ cup grated Parmigiano Reggiano or substitute
2 cups ricotta or vegan substitute
1 Tablespoon julienned fresh sage, or dried
1 Tablespoon fresh parsley, chopped
½ teaspoon minced garlic
2 long neck yellow squash, cut in rounds ¼-inch thick
2 zucchini, cut in rounds ¼-inch thick
1 large yellow onion, sliced thin
12 sheets dry lasagna noodles, cooked al dente
2 cups shredded Fontina cheese or vegan substitute
2 Tablespoons light olive oil

This was one of the first dishes my mom made for Harley. I think it was for one of our first Christmas dinners together, when she was struggling to find interesting vegetarian dishes he would enjoy. This one was a keeper! My mom is an intrepid (and aesthetically driven) chef, and she baked this in a lovely, colorful Dutch oven, but that can be intimidating. You can very easily make this in a traditional roasting pan and not worry about the vessel.

METHOD

1. Mix all sauce ingredients together over low heat until melted and creamy. Set aside.
2. Preheat oven to 450°F.
3. In a medium mixing bowl stir together ricotta, sage, parsley, garlic, and season with salt and pepper to taste. Set aside.
4. In another large bowl, toss yellow squash, zucchini and 1 Tablespoon olive oil, salt and pepper. Arrange in a single layer on a lightly oiled baking sheet. Roast in the oven until lightly browned, about 15–20 minutes, flipping once to brown the second side. Return the zucchini and squash to the bowl.
5. In an oval Dutch oven (or frying pan if you are using a regular baking pan for the lasagna) sauté the onion slices in 1 Tablespoon olive oil until lightly browned. Toss in with the cooked zucchini and yellow squash.
6. Reduce oven temperature to 400°F.
7. a. Spread ½ cup of pumpkin sauce on the bottom of the Dutch oven.
   b. Put a single layer of lasagna noodles over the sauce.
   c. Add ½ cup ricotta in dollops over the noodles.
   d. Layer on 1 cup of the vegetables.
   e. Then spread ½ cup of the pumpkin sauce over the vegetables.
   f. Top with 1 cup of the shredded Fontina cheese.
   g. Repeat layers until top layer is just noodles, sauce and Fontina cheese.
   h. Cut the lasagna in portions before baking (makes it easier to serve once cooked).
8. Bake 45–50 minutes until browned and bubbly. Let the lasagna rest for about 15 minutes before serving.

Serve with a butter lettuce salad and perhaps lentil or minestrone soup.

VEGETARIAN CHILI

SERVES MANY

INGREDIENTS

4 Tablespoons light olive oil
2 medium red onions, chopped
5 cloves garlic, minced
1½ Tablespoons chile powder
1½ Tablespoons ground cumin
1 Tablespoon paprika
1 teaspoon cayenne pepper
1 teaspoon crushed jalapeño or 1 small diced fresh jalapeño
1 cup chopped red bell pepper
1 cup chopped yellow bell pepper
3 carrots, peeled and chopped in rounds
2 celery stalks, chopped
1 (15-ounce) can black beans
1 (15-ounce) can garbanzo beans (chickpeas)
2 (15-ounce) cans diced tomatoes
¼ cup tomato paste
2½ cups vegetable stock
1 cup fresh cilantro, chopped
1 Tablespoon lime juice
grated cheddar and/or sour cream optional at the end

I learned to make chili as an adult. It was never a part of my childhood food experience; though my father loved it, my mother never made it. While I know die-hard chili lovers believe a vegetarian chili can't compete with a meat chili, I beg to differ. I have had both and I have made both, and I think the key to great chili is the spice.

METHOD

1. In a large stock pot (about 16 quarts), heat the olive oil and add the onion. Cook for about 3 minutes, then add the garlic, chili powder, cumin, paprika, cayenne and jalapeño. Sauté while constantly stirring.
2. Add the bell pepper, carrots, celery, and mix all together, for about 5 minutes.
3. Add the beans and mix together, then add the tomatoes and tomato paste. Mix it all together then pour the vegetable stock. Cook over low-medium heat with the lid on.
4. Allow to simmer for at least 40 minutes, checking on it every 15 minutes, and stir it so nothing sticks to the bottom. You can always add more vegetable stock if you need to keep it all simmering and blending together.
5. Before serving, squirt the lime in and mix well. And when you serve, sprinkle with the chopped fresh cilantro. Many people add cheese and sour cream to chili; please go for it if you like.

This is hearty, so serve with a light salad and chips and guacamole (recipe on page 128).

soups and salads

Classic Greek Salad
Dal (*the best you've ever had*)
Roasted Curried Corn Chowder
Gazpacho Soup
Warm French Lentil Salad
Fennel and Parmigiano Reggiano Salad
Caprese Salad
Roasted Sweet Corn Summer Salad
Roasted Curried Squash Soup
Simple Butter Lettuce Salad
(with Harley's Favorite Vinaigrette)
Classic Caesar Salad
German Cucumber Salad
Minestrone
Stumble Upon Acorn Soup

There are so many wonderful soups and salads that it is hard to leave any out of this book, but what I have included are some of my very favorites. Maybe if this book does well, I will have another edition and include some more (hint hint)!

Years ago, my father hit a certain age and proclaimed he was "done with salad!" In his words, "after eating a lifetime of salad, it just doesn't interest me anymore." My father had a unique way not only with words, but pretty much everything. I thought the notion of being "done with" an entire genre of food was hilarious. He was black or white in his proclamations, and I knew he wasn't actually done with them, it would just take something really special to excite those world-weary tastebuds again—like these recipes you are about to try.

GREEK SALAD

SERVES 4

INGREDIENTS

* A medium-size plastic or glass container (about 32 oz.) to mix the dressing and topping

Dressing

3 Tablespoons best quality extra-virgin olive oil
2 Tablespoons red wine vinegar
1 teaspoon Dijon mustard
1 teaspoon mild organic raw honey or agave
1 teaspoon cracked black pepper

The salad

1 cup (10–15 depending on size) plump, hopefully organic, super sweet cherry tomatoes (if you need to substitute other types of tomatoes make sure you have 1 cup when diced)
1 medium English cucumber or 4 little Persian cucumbers, chopped in cubes
½ cup green olives, pitted and diced
½ red pepper, chopped about the size of the cucumber
1 shallot, halved and thinly sliced
1 teaspoon capers
½ teaspoon crushed red pepper
3 heads organic romaine lettuce, cleaned, thoroughly dried, and chopped
sea salt to taste
½ cup best quality fresh feta cheese (no crumbles) (substitute with vegan feta if desired) — LEAVE THIS ON THE SIDE to toss in when you are ready to serve.

Note: *I dice about 1 Tablespoon of Sicilian anchovies to add to my salad, because I eat fish. I keep them separate in a small dish so Harley can make disgusted faces at me while we are eating.*

I, like most New Yorkers, have had every diner version of Greek salad imaginable: from feta that tasted like cardboard, huge tasteless wedges of unripe tomatoes and canned black olives, to the sublime French feta elevated version I had at my local brasserie a couple of blocks from my apartment in Paris when I was 18. I keep revisiting the Greek salad in spite of the largely shitty versions out there, because when done right it is a sublime combination of fabulous flavors of which I never tire. This pup is my version, taking all the best I've had and making it my own. I have decided that the best way to really infuse the salad with the flavors I love is to mix all the ingredients (besides the feta) with the dressing and let it all marinate before I toss it on the lettuce. Sound weird, but try it, you won't go back. And speaking of feta, there are many amazing Greek fetas, but I happen to love Danish feta.

METHOD

1. Mix the dressing ingredients in the plastic container.
2. Add all the ingredients besides the lettuce and feta to the container. *Shake it like a Polaroid picture*...and allow to rest.
3. Clean and chop the lettuce.

*I was taught in Italy that you don't put the salt in the salad dressing, you salt the lettuce before you dress it. I liked that idea. I use a Himalayan pink salt grinder and grind some flakes while I toss the clean salad by hand in the bowl.

4. Give another shake to your Greek concoction and dump it on top of the lettuce. Crumble up the feta or substitute by hand and sprinkle it all over the place.

Toss, serve, delish.

Serve it with toasted bread with a crunchy crust (if in NYC, my all-time fave is Rose & Joe's semolina with sesame seeds from Astoria Queens).

DAL

SERVES 4

INGREDIENTS

1 Tablespoon peanut oil
(substitute with corn or avocado oil)
2 teaspoons ground cumin
1 teaspoon fennel seeds
1 teaspoon black mustard seeds
1 medium shallot, chopped
1 teaspoon Madras curry powder
½ hot green pepper (jalapeño or habañero), diced. Flesh only.
¾ cup red lentils, picked through and rinsed
3⅓ cups water
pinch of red pepper powder
1 teaspoon turmeric powder
2 teaspoons garam masala
1 teaspoon hot curry powder, more or less to taste
herb salt (or just sea salt) to taste

This is by far the best recipe for dal that I have ever tasted, and I have been going to a bazillion Indian restaurants in NYC and abroad since I was a child. I could eat this like soup.

METHOD

1. Heat the peanut oil in a medium saucepan and brown the cumin and fennel seeds.
2. Add the mustard seeds, onion, chile and curry leaves; sauté. Be careful not to let it smoke.
3. Add the lentils, chili powder, turmeric, hot curry powder and garam masala, and cover with water.
   Simmer on low for about 30 minutes, stirring occasionally.
   Make sure it does not overcook and stick to the bottom.
   Leave it longer if need be, but know that the lentils will disintegrate and become very soupy—which is fine because this dal recipe is liquid-y.
   The lentils will not be identifiable as separate lentils at the end.

Serve with anything Indian and definitely with basmati rice.
YOU WILL LOVE THIS.

ROASTED CURRIED CORN CHOWDER

SERVES MANY

INGREDIENTS

4 ears of corn, shucked
1 teaspoon butter and 1 teaspoon olive oil (or substitute with 2 teaspoons olive oil and no butter)
1 whole yellow onion, coarsely chopped
1 jalapeño pepper, de-seeded and diced
3 cups vegetable stock (hopefully your own)
1 can coconut milk (reduced fat if you prefer)
1 teaspoon ground thyme
1 clove garlic, minced
½ teaspoon honey or agave
1 teaspoon minced ginger
1 Tablespoon mild Madras curry powder
1½ teaspoons sea salt and ground pepper to taste
4 Yukon Gold potatoes, cubed - 1-inch

"You do know cellulite is one of the main ingredients in corn chowder"
— Stanley Tucci, *The Devil Wears Prada*

This is one of the best lines EVER from any film, and although I adore Stanley Tucci, this is simply not true...at least not for my corn chowder! There is no heavy cream, no cheese, and you can take out the butter and only use olive oil if you prefer. And feel free to use reduced-fat coconut milk; it will still taste rich and delicious *without the cellulite*.

METHOD

1. Preheat the oven to 425°F.
2. Roast the ears of corn with nothing on them, on a sheet pan or directly on the oven racks (like I do) for approximately 30 minutes, turning them a few times so the corn browns a bit on each side. You want to see some kernels turning brown but not burnt.
3. Remove the corn with tongs and set aside to cool. Once cool, cut the kernels from the ears directly into a bowl with a sharp knife.
4. In a large heavy pot add the butter/olive oil and sauté the onion. Add all other ingredients (including corn, of course) and simmer... forever. You can make this in a crockpot if you have one or know what that means. I don't so I make it on the stove—*slow and low, that is the tempo*. Stir on occasion. The flavors should take about an hour to really meld and become creamy and delicious.

GAZPACHO

SERVES 6

INGREDIENTS

- 8 plum tomatoes, or 20 cherry tomatoes, chopped
- 2 cucumbers, halved and seeded but not peeled, chopped into 1-inch cubes
- 1 large red bell pepper, seeded, chopped into 1-inch cubes
- 1 small red onion, chopped into 1-inch cubes
- 2 garlic cloves, minced
- 2 cups tomato juice
- 1 Tablespoon white/red/Champagne wine vinegar (not balsamic)
- 1 Tablespoon olive oil (flavorful is fine)
- 3 Tablespoons chopped fresh cilantro
- 1 Tablespoon chopped fresh Italian parsley
- 1 serrano or poblano chile, seeded and diced
- Ground salt & pepper to taste

Gazpacho, like Greek salad, is another simple dish that can go so wrong, yet I will still muscle through it. I've had it taste like salsa, like marinara sauce, like chunks of tasteless nothing…AND then, I have had it taste so sublime that it just *keeps pulling me back in* for one more hopeful try.

Given all the pain I have suffered, I figured I might as well give it a whirl myself. I think this version is delightful.

Oh yeah, and as for serving gazpacho, it is definitely one of those "cold soups" like vichyssoise, that you can be fancy and serve in a little demitasse with hors d'oeuvres at a party and be all super-sophisto—because it never disappoints ☺

METHOD

1. Roughly chop the tomatoes and add a little salt to them in a bowl. Let them sit alone, by themselves in the corner until they cry…LOL. In other words, let the water come out a bit before adding them to the other veggies below.
2. Working with one vegetable at a time (cucumbers, bell peppers, onion, then parsley, cilantro and chiles last) add it to your food processor. Pulse until coarse chopped; do not over-blend. Add each individual vegetable to a large bowl, then process the next one.
   Last, add the tomatoes (without the water that came out of them).
3. After each vegetable is processed, combine in a large bowl and add garlic and tomato juice. Add vinegar, oil, salt and pepper. Mix well and chill before serving.

Best to serve the next day once the flavors are more intense.
Serve cold (of course).

WARM FRENCH LENTIL SALAD

SERVES 4

The lentil is a sublime little legume. Is it just me, but isn't it amazing that there are pink and yellow and French and green and black lentils? Lentils ALWAYS make me think of *The Young Ones*' character Neil the hippie, always cooking lentils for their impoverished student household. It was a British comedy I used to watch as a young teenager in the middle of the night when it finally came to the States as a rerun, on MTV. I LOVED it, and arguably it was my first real introduction to the lentil. They were not a "thing" in my house growing up, so I came to them late. But I have more than made up for my lentil-less youth with gusto!

INGREDIENTS

1 cup of green or black lentils, rinsed and picked over
2-3 cups vegetable stock (salt to taste if unsalted)
1 medium tomato (about ¾ cup) or about 6 or 7 cherry tomatoes, diced
1 medium shallot, diced
2 small Persian cucumbers (or 1 small English cucumber), diced
1 small yellow pepper, diced
1 Tablespoon chopped fresh Italian (flat leaf) parsley
salt to taste, fresh ground black pepper

*crumbled best quality chevre or vegan substitute or none at all

Dressing

3 Tablespoons best quality extra-virgin olive oil
2 Tablespoons balsamic vinegar (sometimes I prefer red wine vinegar for this)
1 teaspoon Dijon mustard
1 teaspoon mild organic raw honey
1 teaspoon cracked black pepper

**you can always add more dressing per your taste*

METHOD

1. Bring the stock to a boil in a 2-quart saucepan, then add the lentils. Lower heat to medium-low. Simmer the lentils until they are tender—can be anywhere between 15 to 30 minutes depending on the lentil. Drain them then set aside until cool.
2. In a large mixing bowl add the remaining salad ingredients and toss with the lentils.

Mix the dressing, then toss with the salad.

Place all in a serving bowl and serve. It's a perfect summer dish.

FENNEL AND PARMIGIANO REGGIANO SALAD

SERVES 4

INGREDIENTS

3 small fennel bulbs
(larger bulbs tend to have tough outer layers, but will work if you peel them away)
½ cup shavings of best quality Parmigiano Reggiano
(I use a carrot peeler to shave the cheese)
2 Tablespoons best quality extra-virgin olive oil
1 Tablespoon red wine vinegar
Salt and ground pepper

This is the simplest salad ever, it's almost disarming...if a salad can be disarming. I love raw fennel and I love aged Parmigiano Reggiano. Years ago in Italy, I had this salad and was amazed by how delicious it was, and how little there was to it. As usual, with the best Italian food, it is really all about the quality of the ingredients: no complicated sauces, just fresh whole tasty foods.

Digression Alert: I can't help but remember when I first had this salad, and I must tell you about it. I was in a really bad—read *super touristy*—pizza place in Florence when I was about 20. Florence, in my opinion, is no longer Italian; it is a world heritage site, an open-air museum that is in the custody and care of the Italians. As such, you can get yourself a "big salad" and ketchup. In other words, you CAN get a very bad meal in Florence (Venice too).

Sorry, my Italian peeps, but these are the facts, and you know it. At any rate, waiting for a truly horrible pizza, my ex and I order a fennel salad—and despite the misery of the pizza, the salad was insanely delicious. But the truly memorable part, what I will always think of when I think of fennel salad, is the piranhas. We were seated next to a large fish tank filled with piranhas—about 30. During the entire meal, all of them, except one, were staring menacingly at my ex, while one lone savage was staring in the other direction—right at me, literally making eye contact. It was unsettling, but a wonderful memory nonetheless.

METHOD:

1. Wash fennel well and pull off the tough outer layers. Slice the fennel very thin—a mandoline would be great for this, but watch your fingers!
2. Place in a mixing bowl. Add the shaved cheese and grind salt and pepper to taste. Toss with oil and vinegar and that's it.

Yes, it is that simple. The flavors are so powerful and mix so beautifully together there is nothing else needed.

CAPRESE SALAD

SERVES 4

INGREDIENTS

4 medium ripe tomatoes
½ cup fresh basil leaves
1 ball fresh mozzarella
(I prefer buffalo, but excellent quality cow milk mozzarella exists)
2 Tablespoons extra virgin olive oil
1 Tablespoon balsamic vinegar

It is such a simple staple and yet so often ruined with too much balsamic or roasted peppers or crappy tomatoes; but done well, it is a perfect summer treat. This is one of those dishes that completely depends on the freshness and flavor of summer tomatoes and the quality of the cheese.

I like using Kumato tomatoes unless I have farmers market heirloom or home-grown tomatoes to work with. No need for fancy aged versions, just regular balsamic works best here; a fine "real" balsamic vinegar should cost between $12–20—super aged ones can cost in the hundreds.

METHOD

1. Slice the tomatoes about ¼-inch wide and place in a bowl with a dusting of ground salt. Let them sit for about 20 minutes to "fare aqua" (literally "make water").
2. While that's happening, slice the cheese about the same width.
3. Remove the tomatoes from their liquid. Arrange the cheese and tomatoes alternating; I like to do it in circles toward the middle of a plate.
4. Drizzle with oil and balsamic (add salt as needed, but if the cheese is salted and the tomatoes already were, you will not need any more salt). I like to snip thin strips of the basil leaves and toss them all over the composition.

Simple summer perfection.

ROASTED SWEET CORN SUMMER SALAD

SERVES 4

INGREDIENTS

2 Tablespoons extra virgin olive oil
1 Tablespoon basic balsamic vinegar
4 ears fresh sweet corn
1 small shallot, diced
½ cup fresh basil leaves, chopped coarsely
salt and pepper

In my opinion, one of life's great pleasures is summer corn. Some people wash it, some people do not. It reminds me of Julia Child famously quoting a French chef who explained why washing a chicken is not necessary before roasting it: "If it can kill me after it's done, it deserves to!" or something to that effect…I love this so much! But pesticides are real and clingy, so if you are not sure how your corn was farmed, wash it. I make this recipe religiously every summer.

METHOD

Preheat the oven to 400°F.

1. Peel the corn.
2. Roast the corn for about 20 to 30 minutes depending how hot your oven runs. The kernels should start to brown in places, and when that happens it's ready. Take out the corn with tongs and set aside in a mixing bowl to cool.
3. Once cool cut the kernels into the bowl using a sharp knife. Add in all the other ingredients and combine well. Add more salt and pepper as needed.

Serve at room temperature. It is heavenly.

ROASTED CURRIED SQUASH SOUP

SERVES 4–6

INGREDIENTS

1 large (1½–2 pounds) butternut squash, roasted, peeled and seeded and cut into chunks
3 Tablespoons light olive oil
1 teaspoon butter or substitute
1 large yellow onion, or 3 shallots, diced
1 Tablespoon Madras curry powder
2 teaspoons whole black mustard seeds or ¼ teaspoon mustard powder
½ teaspoon ground cumin
1 Tablespoon fresh ginger, minced
4 cups vegetable stock
1 (13-ounce) can organic coconut milk, or light coconut milk
1 teaspoon salt, or more to taste
ground pepper, to taste

I do love butternut squash soup. And there are so many varieties: with sage, curry, savory or sweet. Butternut squash is sublime. I go a few ways with this soup but tend to lean on the curry side of things. NOTE: I have also added kabocha and now acorn squash to this recipe and it works beautifully.

METHOD

1. Preheat oven to 375°F.
2. Place your whole butternut (or other squash) in a baking pan. Let it cook for about 15–20 minutes. Cut in half and set aside to cool.
3. In a 5-quart Dutch oven, or 8-quart large stock pot, heat the oil and butter, sauté the onion and all the spices including the ginger.
   NOTE: if using a stock pot make sure to move the ingredients around a bit so they do not burn. Mix constantly. Add the chunks of butternut squash and mix well. Add the stock and low boil. Let it cook down, reducing the volume of liquid, for about 15–20 minutes. Turn off the heat and let it rest until it's just warm and you can blend it all.
4. Add solid contents with a slotted spoon to a blender or food processor and blend in batches. Alternatively, you can use an immersion blender right in the pot. Move the creamy smooth soup back to the pot.
5. Once you've blended all the chunks add the coconut milk and bring to a boil once again.
6. Check seasoning for salt and pepper and maybe you can add a little cayenne to give it some heat (optional).
   ALSO: if you want to add a bit more sweetness, you can squeeze a little agave.

SIMPLE BUTTER LETTUCE (WITH HARLEY'S FAVORITE VINAIGRETTE)

SERVES 4

I was late to the butter lettuce party. Growing up with an Italian mother, we ate radicchio, arugula, maybe some spinach and romaine.

But, like all delicious foods I came to later in life, I have embraced its wonderfulness with all of my heart.

I love butter lettuce; it is so delicate and wants such simple flavors to show off its creamy delicacy. Harley and I love it with a shallot vinaigrette.

INGREDIENTS

1 head butter lettuce, washed and dried completely. If the leaves are large, feel free to tear them a little so you can eat the salad without looking like a savage.

Dressing

2 Tablespoons extra virgin olive oil
1 Tablespoon champagne vinegar (or other good white wine vinegar)
½ small shallot, diced
½ Tablespoon Dijon mustard
½ Tablespoon mild flavored honey (more if you prefer it sweeter as Harley does) or agave
salt and pepper

METHOD

Mix the dressing well, adding more honey/agave or salt and pepper as you prefer. Toss with the lettuce, and that's it. I also like to add some thinly sliced cucumber, but not necessary.

*I also sometimes add marinated sheep's cheese and toasted pignoli nuts, for an absolutely dreamy, creamy situation.

CLASSIC CAESAR SALAD

SERVES 4, *OR 1 IF YOU ARE ME*

INGREDIENTS

2 heads of romaine lettuce, washed and dried completely
½ cup Parmigiano Reggiano, finely grated
1 egg yolk, raw
2½ Tablespoons extra virgin olive oil
1 teaspoon vegan or vegetarian Worcestershire sauce
2 Tablespoons chopped fresh Italian parsley
1 teaspoon Dijon mustard
1 teaspoon capers
1 clove garlic, finely chopped
4-5 anchovy fillets, in oil*
1 Tablespoon ground black pepper

*For vegetarian, I would reccomend a blend of Tamari, miso paste, and a bit of water to get it to a saucier consistency—I have made this for Harley without them—but I ALWAYS use anchovies in mine.

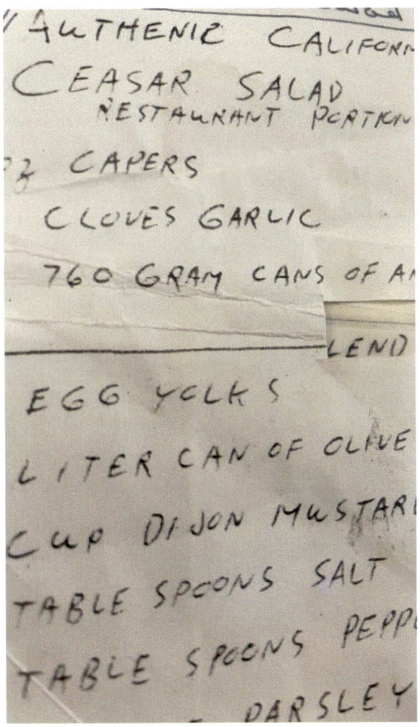

This is admittedly not a vegetarian recipe, but it is still very close to my heart. My father could not cook much of anything. He married a great cook and left it at that. But he loved food, from caviar to peanut butter and everything in between. He was more of a gourmand than a gourmet, but he taught me so much about so many different cuisines that it's hard to place him in any category. In his quest for "the" perfect Caesar salad, he bribed a waiter at the old Ginger Man near Lincoln Center on the West Side—his own way of searching for "authenticity."

Together we converted the restaurant quantities in his handwritten recipe to human scale and, as in all things, over the years I have made it authentically mine. This recipe is for four normal people, but sometimes when Harley is on tour, I make this for only me, and with a toasted piece of Italian semolina bread covered with sesame seeds and a glass (or two) of Barolo…heaven.

METHOD

1. Heat the oven to 250°F and toast your bread.
2. In a large mixing bowl add the egg, oil and then all of the other ingredients (minus the lettuce), mixing well with a fork, until it is all creamy and chunky.
3. Chop the lettuce into 1-inch strips and add all of the lettuce to bowl. I mix the dressing up from the bottom and work it into the lettuce slowly and methodically; it is like a ritual.

That's it. It's the best. The Ginger Man and most recipes call for croutons, but if you are having crusty, crunchy warm bread, who needs them? Add if you choose.

GERMAN CUCUMBER SALAD

SERVES 4

INGREDIENTS

3 medium cucumbers, peeled and thinly sliced into rounds
⅓ cup chopped fresh dill
1 large or 2 small shallots, thinly sliced
3 Tablespoons light olive oil
3 Tablespoons apple cider vinegar
1½ teaspoons honey or agave
Salt and pepper to taste

I was raised in part by a German nanny. Yes…with all of what that comes with (insane devotion, strictness, indulgence, nostalgic schlock, marzipan…the works). She was from Munich, and I adored her. Her name was Johanna Schwarz but as little babies my brother and I called her "Petunia." She came as a baby nanny when I was born and stayed with us until she passed away when I was ten. I miss her still.

My mother is an exceptional cook. My nanny's repertoire wasn't so extensive. Petunia's best meals included red cherry Jell-O (with vanilla ice cream), potato pancakes, and German cucumber salad. As it so happens, I LOVE potato pancakes and German cucumber salad, so we were in business.

This recipe is not hers; she made it from memory and never wrote it down. So I have created my own based on the taste, which I remember in my soul.

METHOD

1. Add the cucumbers, shallots and dill (if using) in a deep bowl.
2. Add all other ingredients and mix well: cucumber, shallots and dressing.

NOTE: Ideally this should stay in a container overnight, so the cucumber really breaks down and softens with the vinegar. Once it does this chemical dance, you will be delighted with the results, both the texture and flavor. And you can let it rest for several days for even more textural breakdown.

MINESTRONE

SERVES MANY

INGREDIENTS

4 Tablespoons extra virgin olive oil, divided
1 medium red onion, chopped in 1-inch pieces
4 cloves garlic, pressed
½ teaspoon dried oregano
½ teaspoon dried thyme
2 medium carrots, peeled and chopped
2 medium stalks celery, 1-inch pieces
2 cups chopped (in 1-inch pieces) seasonal vegetables like tomatoes, fennel, golden zucchini, delicata squash
¼ cup tomato paste
1 28-ounce can diced tomatoes with their liquid, OR 2 cups fresh tomatoes, diced
4 cups vegetable stock
2 cups water
1 teaspoon fine sea salt
ground black pepper to taste
2 dried bay leaves
⅛ teaspoon red pepper flakes
1 cup orecchiette, elbow or small shell pasta
1½ cups cooked garbanzo beans (chickpeas)
2 cups baby spinach, chopped
1 Tablespoon basil pesto
*I make my own pesto and freeze it in small batches. But, you can substitute store-bought jarred pesto sauce.
1 2-inch chunk of Parmigiano Reggiano rind (if available)
Extra freshly grated Parmigiano Reggiano for garnish

Harley loves minestrone soup. I make it, my mom makes it, and he loves both iterations.

There is a restaurant that my mom and stepdad used to go to on the West Side. It was a romantic place for them and then became the main family-gathering restaurant for many years.

Oddly, about a year into our relationship, Harley met me in Midtown after work in the middle of a serious blizzard—one of those legendary NYC blizzards where you can't see 20 feet ahead even though you are essentially in Times Square…and we were! We wandered west and found ourselves on 45th Street and 8th Avenue, trudging through the snow, blinded, frozen and hungry.

We had to stop, and so we turned to see what was near and walked into a restaurant in the lower level of a brownstone. Once inside, we shook off the madness and found ourselves in that very same restaurant—besides one other couple, we were the only people there. It was so warm and so inviting; it was romantic. Harley ordered minestrone soup—and thereafter, every single time we ate there (even in the middle of summer).

Every culture has some version of minestrone soup. *Una Minestra*—literally, a soup—and in my family, like in Italy, minestrone has come to mean whatever vegetables you have on hand that you don't want to go bad…and that makes sense. This is by far one of Harley's all-time favorite soups. In a perfect world I would use these veggies below, but substitute with what you have on hand.

METHOD

1. Add olive oil to a large pot, heat to medium and sauté chopped red onion until translucent.
2. Add garlic and dried oregano and thyme, mix until fragrant.
3. Add all of the chopped vegetables and coat well with onion/garlic mixture.
4. Add tomatoes, stock, water, salt and pepper, bay leaves, and red pepper flakes. Bring to a boil and then simmer on low for about half an hour.
5. Stir in the pesto, add the garbanzo beans and parmesan rind. Continue cooking on low for about an hour. The liquid will reduce making the flavors blend in the most heavenly way. Taste to check if it is rich enough to your liking.
6. If you plan to freeze the leftovers, cook your pasta separately or it will defrost mushy. So cook whatever pasta you like—I like orecchiette—as per the package separately, and add to the soup when you are going to serve it.

There should be some sort of crunchy crusted Italian or French bread served with this, in principle (on a cold and stormy winter night if you can conjure that up).

STUMBLE UPON ACORN SQUASH SOUP

SERVES 4

INGREDIENTS

1 acorn squash
3 Tablespoons light olive oil
1 large shallot, chopped
1 Granny Smith apple, peeled, cored, and diced
12 little creamer potatoes (cut in half) or 4 medium Yukon Gold potatoes, cubed
1 Tablespoon crushed sage
1½ teaspoons dried rosemary
3 cups vegetable stock
1 cup creamy almond milk or whole milk
Salt and pepper to taste
2 cups fresh or frozen cheese tortellini

I love when creativity strikes and you have the presence of mind to write down what you did, so you don't have to be a one-hit wonder. This happened recently while I was hoping to make butternut squash soup, only having an acorn squash, and doing a little dance with some surprise ingredients.

You can make this soup as is, or recently I have been using it as the vehicle for a newfangled "*Tortellini in brodo*" which is traditionally made with either chicken or beef stock and cheese or meat tortellini. I make this soup and add cheese tortellini and it is dreamy on a cold winter night.

METHOD

1. Heat the oven to 400°F.
2. Place your acorn squash, whole, on a baking dish and bake for a good 30 minutes. You can turn it over after 20. Once cooked take it out and cut it in half to cool down. I pull out the seeds and save them to roast later ☺ So good.
3. In a large stock pot, add the oil and heat over medium heat. Add the shallot and apple and toss around for about 5 minutes until shallots are translucent and apple is tender. Add the herbs, salt, and pepper to taste, and toss for another 2–3 minutes.
4. Scoop the flesh from the acorn squash into the pot. Stir and mix with the shallot/apple mixture. Add the vegetable stock before anything burns.
5. Add the potatoes to the liquid and bring it all to a gentle boil. Cook like this, stirring every few minutes, for about 20 minutes.
6. It should cook down a bit, then add the almond milk and stir together. After another 10 minutes turn off the heat and let the soup settle.
7. Once it is warm—not too hot—add the solid stuff (I do this with a slotted spoon) to a blender or food processor. Blend until creamy and return batches back to the pot. Alternatively, you can use an immersion blender right in the pot.

The soup should be thick and creamy. You can adjust thickness by letting it cook down more or adding a bit more vegetable stock.

Cook the tortellini separately per the package and add when you serve the soup.

sides and small plates

Wild Rice and Crunchy Tofu
Roasted Fennel Flatbread
Roasted Vegetable Menagerie
Crunchy Hen-of-the-Woods (Maitake) Mushrooms
Simple Sautéed Spinach
Roasted Delicata Squash and Shallots
Vegetable Fried Rice
Classic Stuffed Artichokes
Ricotta Bruschetta
Roasted Rosemary Potatoes
Laura's (Now Famous) Guacamole
My Mom's Outstanding Caponata
Potato Pancakes
Onion Bhaji
Luciana's Trifolata
Summer Borlotti Beans
Roasted Butternut Squash
Wild Mushroom and Arugula Flatbread
Crunchy Cauliflower with Capers
Pesto Stuffed Mushrooms
Jeanne's Knækbrød
Raita
Baba Ghanoush

WILD MUSHROOM FLATBREAD, ROASTED CAULIFLOWER AND CRUNCHY CAPERS (WITH ADDED PASTA)

PESTO STUFFED MUSHROOMS

I love the idea of "small plates." The term is sort of new, trendy and strange, but I have always loved antipasti, tapas, appetizers—whatever you want to call them, in whatever culture, I am a fan of tasting little servings of lots of different things. And conceptually, I think vegetarian and vegan foods lend themselves to this type of eating. The traditional meal, with a big steak or roast bird as the centerpiece and side dishes intended to complement, seems dated and, as we now know, not very healthy.

Some research suggests that eating smaller servings throughout the day, instead of one large meal at any point, is an easier way for our bodies to process food. It may also help keep us in better shape, allowing us to metabolize what we consume more efficiently. Whatever you believe, you will likely not feel as uncomfortably full after your meal.

Again, if you listen to your body, it tells you what it wants and what it does not want. I, for one, can't stand finishing a meal and feeling overly full, distended and in need of a couch. If I can, I prefer eating small portions of delicious foods and coming back for more later if I am still hungry ;)

WILD RICE WITH CRUNCHY TOFU

SERVES 4

INGREDIENTS

1 package of firm or extra-firm tofu
1 Tablespoon ground sage
2 Tablespoons peanut oil
2 Tablespoons olive oil
2 small shallots, or 1 medium
1 small package (about 1 cup) of wild rice (not blended)
2 cups + vegetable stock
1 Tablespoon toasted pignoli nuts
ground salt and pepper

Wild rice is a beautiful thing. I have been eating it all my life and I love it so. My dad was a super fan and my mom made it often to satisfy the need. Since childhood I have had it in salads and soups, creamy and dry and everything in between. For me, "simple" (as you know) is always best…let the deep woodsy flavor speak for itself with little interference.

METHOD

1. Prepare the tofu (as described on pages 129–130) for frying. Along with the salt and pepper, add a bit of the sage to the tofu before you throw it in the pan. I make small 1-cm cubes for this dish. Fry it in the very hot peanut oil so it has time to get really crunchy; set aside on a paper towel.
2. Prepare the rice: I like to start all rice as I would risotto, so I heat the olive oil in a sauce pan and chop the shallots and sauté them until they are translucent. Then add the rice and coat with the oil and shallots. Pour in the vegetable stock.
3. Cook on a low heat, stirring frequently. I keep it covered with the lid a little open. Wild rice takes a long time—around 45 minutes to an hour at least for it to become very tender and the grains themselves have split open. All or most of the stock should have been absorbed by this time. If it looks particularly dry, you may decide to add a bit more stock, then turn off the heat.
4. In a small pan drop in your pignoli nuts, turn up the flame and shake them in the pan. They will burn so fast you will be shocked, so shake them around like you're making popcorn until they are browning. Turn off the heat and quickly dump them in the rice before they burn.
5. Add your crunchy tofu to the mix, stir it all up well and serve warm. So so yummy…I want to eat it right now!

ROASTED FENNEL FLATBREAD

SERVES 2–4

INGREDIENTS

2 Tablespoons olive oil
3 medium fennel bulbs, halved and thinly sliced
2-3 small shallots, peeled and thinly sliced
grated Parmigiano Reggiano (Parmesan or vegan substitute) – about ½ cup
ground salt and pepper to taste
1 package of naan (2 pieces) or 2 round pita (if you can't find the naan). You can also use pizza crust, chickpea or cauliflower variations as well.

Flatbread is great. It's really just a pizza variation, and why not? It is the perfect medium for handheld flavorful bits. I use naan (as here), Brooklyn bakery flatbread, and chickpea and cauliflower pizza crust to make my many flatbread concoctions.

A few key flatbread hints, so you don't experience the same epic fails as me: Don't use anything too wet or too oily—I messed up with pesto, as well as marinara sauce, and it just gets soggy; don't use toppings that are too big so you have to chew or bite them in pieces as you are eating, because you will inevitably pull a big chunk of whatever it is off the bread and onto your shirt; and don't double-starch, carb or over-cheese the situation. The toppings should be distinct from the vehicle and not overtake it. Keep it "SIMPLE." ☺

That said, and a dozen flatbread experiments later, I give you my still-reigning champion:

METHOD

1. Heat oven to 400°F. You will be placing your pan on a lower rack, so check to be sure there's room before the oven gets too hot.
2. In a shallow roasting pan (I use one about 12x24) add olive oil.
3. Add the sliced fennel and shallots to the pan.
   Add salt and pepper to taste. Toss it all with your hands.
4. Place the pan low in the oven so the heat is close and will caramelize the shallots and fennel. Bake for about 20–25 minutes, but check every 10 minutes and toss it all around—you want to make sure nothing burns and it all browns and gets crunchy evenly.
5. Once browned and beautiful, I take the mixture out of the pan and put it in a bowl, take the naan and spread the two pieces on the same pan. Let it cook until they are slightly brown for about 5 to 10 minutes, then pull them out and flip the pieces.
6. Pull out the pan (unless you don't mind working in front of a hot open oven). Evenly distribute the fennel and shallots all over the bread. Cover the fennel/shallots with the cheese; add a little more crushed pepper and back in the oven to brown for about 10 minutes. You want the edges of the bread to start to brown and crisp, so leave it a couple minutes longer if needed.

With a spatula, I remove the pieces and lay them on a clean, dry wood cutting board. Let cool for about 5 minutes and slice into sections with a pizza cutter.
SO GOOD!

ROASTED VEGETABLE MÉLANGE

SERVES 4

INGREDIENTS

2 Tablespoons light olive oil
3 Yukon Gold unpeeled potatoes, sliced into 1-inch pieces
1 medium parsnip, peeled and sliced into 1-inch pieces
1 medium carrot, peeled, sliced into 1-inch pieces
1 medium turnip, peeled, sliced into 1-inch pieces
1 yam or sweet unpeeled potato, sliced into 1-inch pieces
5 sunchokes (if available), sliced into 1-inch pieces
8 small shallots (if too large, use 4 and cut lengthwise in half)
6 cloves garlic, peeled, halved and smashed
1 Tablespoon herbes de Provence
1 teaspoon fresh or dried rosemary
1 teaspoon ground sage
ground salt and pepper to taste

Years ago, friends came over for dinner and, in part, helped prepare it. He and his wife had just bought a place in the South of France and were raving about a winter vegetable dish they had there that sounded absolutely too complicated to me at the time. I was unfamiliar with the taste of the vegetables and spices cooked together, so I was skeptical, as one of them prepared the dish. WOW, was I wrong. I have made it ever since, which is the biggest compliment I can give in the kitchen. It should be noted that precise measurements of these vegetables aren't critical. This is a mélange! Each time you make it, maybe it will be subtly different, but always delicious.

METHOD

Heat oven to 450°F.

1. In a large paella pan or similar oven-ready pan, coat bottom with light olive oil.
   Add all prepared vegetables in the pan.
   Add the herbes de Provence, rosemary, thyme, salt and pepper.
   Toss together with your hands and coat.
2. Roast for 20 minutes, periodically shaking the pan or stirring to help the vegetables cook evenly.
3. After another 15 minutes toss it all around again. We want everything browned and crunchy and fragrant and delicious, so keep going until you have those results.

This is a warm and comforting winter dish.

CRUNCHY HEN OF THE WOODS (MAITAKE) MUSHROOMS

SERVES 2

INGREDIENTS

1 pound maitake mushrooms (they're expensive and they shrink when you cook them, FYI)
1 Tablespoon olive oil
ground sea salt or ground Himalayan pink salt to taste
About 1 teaspoon ground black pepper

I don't know why these are so good. I am a huge mushroom person; I love shiitake, oyster, cremini, porcini, morels, enoki…it goes on forever. Harley, not so much. In fact, when we met, he wouldn't eat any mushrooms at all. I had to convince him that a truffle (which he loved immediately) wasn't a mushroom. Then one day, at a local place with a great and adventurous chef, Hen of the Woods appeared on the menu. They came as an appetizer cooked in some indescribably delicious way with polenta. He fell in love and declared, as of that day, he would eat Hen of the Woods (or maitake) mushrooms all day long.

At that same restaurant we became friendly with that talented young chef—and like it was yesterday, I recall when Anthony Bourdain died, and we ate there the first time after that horrible news. The chef knew Harley was close to Tony and he prepared a special "mourning dish" for us, which was special to his culture. It was made up of many root and other vegetables that grow close to the ground. It is symbolic of our permanent connection and ultimate return to the earth. It was moving and unforgettable.

Hen of the Woods are not that easy to find and, as of now, I get them at my weekly farmers market, at Eli's or from Fresh Direct. I acknowledge it is easier to find what you want in NYC than in most places. So if you are lucky enough to come across these beauties, please try them. They are not cheap—but they are worth it.

The way I make them, they are the perfect crunchy snack. I could eat them alone with a good glass of Sancerre and call it a night.

METHOD

Heat the oven to 450°F.

This is so easy it's hardly really cooking:

1. Lightly coat a shallow roasting or sheet pan with olive oil.
2. Remove only the harder base of the mushroom (I freeze them with other veggies scraps to make vegetable stock).
3. Tear the fronds apart into strips. No need to wash them unless they are really dirty, and then they must be completely dry before you roast them. Don't crowd them! Make sure they have a bit of oil and salt and spread them out.
4. I roast them on a low rack in the oven so they are close to the heat underneath. They cook (and burn) fast, so watch them and move them in the pan every 5–10 minutes. They will start browning and getting crunchy quickly. Make sure you are checking until they are crunchy.

Once done they are like dark little chips of wonderfulness. I don't know how else to describe them.

They taste remarkably like bacon, just say'n. I have never tasted a vegetable so close to bacon—so if you decide to make your own version of a Beyond Burger, I highly recommend that you toss a handful of these beauties onto it to transform it into an existential burger experience (with no meat).

SIMPLE SAUTÉED SPINACH

SERVES 2

INGREDIENTS

2 pounds cleaned baby spinach
1 Tablespoon olive oil
2 medium cloves garlic
ground salt and pepper to taste

Fresh spinach disappears when you cook it, so 2 pounds becomes a small bowl. I usually just do more. But the gist is the same.

Why is it so good? I can't answer this question. But I can tell you that as a teenage wild child in the city I would regularly wind up at Lucky Strike on Grand and West Broadway at 3 a.m. trying to get my underage self un-drunk with friends, eating roasted rosemary potatoes and sautéed spinach. Maybe that is why it stays so near and dear to my culinary heart. Perhaps that is why each time I make this simple, healthy delight, I am transported back there…minus the hangover.

METHOD

1. Slice your garlic into pieces you can see—so you can take it out if you want to, like those northern Italians ;)
2. Add the oil to a nonstick pan; heat for a few minutes and add the garlic. As it starts to brown add salt and pepper and then add the first pile of spinach, essentially overflowing the pan, and try to hold it in while leaves fall onto the stove and the floor.
3. With tongs I wrangle the leaves into the pan as they quickly shrink. Continue adding fresh leaves as more room is made in the pan. As they cook keep moving the leaves and turning them to coat them with the garlic and the oil.
4. It shouldn't take more than 10 minutes for it all to be wilted and perfect. Add a bit more salt and pepper (and then adjust later as needed).

The key to this is now removing the excess liquid (water released from the cooked spinach).

I do this by gathering the spinach against the side of the pan and pressing it hard over and over while turning it and holding the pan on an angle, so all the liquid gathers on the other side. Carefully either pull the spinach out or dump the liquid in the sink.

I move the spinach to a plate and sprinkle with Parmigiano Reggiano (or not…up to you).

ROASTED DELICATA SQUASH AND SHALLOTS

SERVES 2

INGREDIENTS

2 delicata squash (medium, at least 7")
1½ Tablespoons olive oil
2 large shallots, thinly sliced
ground salt and pepper to taste

This was another local restaurant find, because for as long as I can remember, I thought delicata squash was a type of decorative squash. I was happily wrong. The chef made it lightly fried like tempura with some sort of mustard-based cream which was intoxicating. But as usual, in line with the Italian roots, I simplified and let the food just speak (a.k.a. laziness).

These are wonderfully seasonal. You will find them in Northeast farmers markets in late September to mid-November/December. It gives us something to look forward to each year—as we should. And remarkably, this squash is easy to cut, unlike so many others.

METHOD

1. Heat oven to 450°F.
2. Coat a shallow roasting or sheet pan with oil.
3. Wash the squash and slice them in half, then in quarters. Scoop the guts and seeds out (a melon scoop works SO well, as does a grapefruit spoon).
4. Once cleaned, slice in thin strips.
5. Slice your shallot into thin strips.
6. Toss the shallots and squash in the pan. Move them around with your hands to make sure they have been lightly coated with oil. Add salt and pepper to taste.
7. Place in the oven on a low shelf close to the heat. Toss these well about every 10 minutes. I actually get so neurotic about these pups that sometimes I turn them with a fork one at a time because I like them perfectly caramelized. No need to go as cray cray as me though.

You will know when they are perfect because they will be brown and smell delicious.

VEGETABLE FRIED RICE

SERVES 4

I love basic Chinese-American fried rice and I decided not too long ago that if I can cook Indian—*without looking at a recipe*—I CERTAINLY can make killer vegetable fried rice. This is a simple recipe which has some of my culinary "style."

P.S. I often make this dish with black rice; why, you ask? It all goes back to one of my all-time favorite films: *The Cook, The Thief, His Wife and Her Lover* and…"black foods." *Go with me, people:* when asked why black foods on the menu were always the highest priced, the chef explained, not in these exact words: people want to control death, we are helpless toward death. Black reminds people of death, and eating death is satisfying because it gives people the feeling that they have control over death. *I love it!* Sold. I cook with black foods whenever I can to create the illusion of controlling death.

INGREDIENTS

1 cup jasmine or black rice (this can also always be made with leftover rice—it is a great reason to save extra rice and use it)
Vegetable stock to use per the package directions of liquid per cup of rice
2 Tablespoons peanut oil
1 small yellow onion
1 small sweet bell pepper (red, orange or yellow)
1 head of broccoli, florets cut very small
1 teaspoon minced garlic (use a garlic press)
1 teaspoon minced fresh ginger
1 teaspoon red pepper flakes
3 scallions, thinly sliced
3 Tablespoons soy sauce
½ cup frozen peas
1 scallion
2 Tablespoons toasted sesame oil
ground salt and pepper to taste

NOTE: If making this in fall, I will use about a cup of small cubed delicata squash as well—tastes so good.

METHOD

1. Follow the package directions for the rice and add a few drops of toasted sesame oil to the boiling vegetable stock. Do not overcook the rice; it will continue to cook a little in the hot pan with the veggies.
2. At the same time steam the broccoli. It should be super-fast because the pieces are small, so watch it so it doesn't get mushy—you want little crispy florets.
3. In a nonstick pan, heat peanut and toasted sesame oil and sauté the yellow onion, pepper flakes and bell pepper about 5 minutes on medium heat, then add the garlic. Add the crunchy broccoli (and delicata squash if using), the ginger and then the cooked rice. Stir it all together well and add the soy sauce. Let it cook on pretty high heat because ideally the rice will start to stick to the pan a little and "fry"… oh yeah. Toward the end of this process add the frozen peas. They will cook quickly and not get mushy if you add toward the end.
4. Toss the cooked rice with chopped raw scallions.
   You may want to add a little more soy sauce per your taste.

CLASSIC STUFFED ARTICHOKES

SERVES 4

INGREDIENTS

4 medium artichokes, cleaned and outer leaves discarded
3 Tablespoons olive oil
2 cloves garlic
½ Tablespoon crushed red pepper
1 Tablespoon fresh oregano (chopped) or 1 teaspoon dry
1 Tablespoon fresh Italian parsley, chopped
1 cup panko or plain breadcrumbs
1½ cups vegetable broth
½ cup dry white wine (optional—replace with more broth if not using)
ground black pepper and salt to taste

NOTE: Breadcrumbs matter. The quality of your breadcrumbs will be a game-changer in this recipe. If you can buy "homemade" from a bakery or elsewhere, or can grate them yourself, you will be so happy with the result. The finer the better.

Stuffed artichokes were heavily featured in one of the first food memories I have with my stepsons. 2012 was a really rough year for Harley and his boys…pretty rough for me, as well, but we spent a lot of time together trying to have fun and distract ourselves from all the madness we had going on in our lives. That always involved food. One of our favorite places was a little local Italian that had changed owners a few times in my lifetime but, in those years, had become our neighborhood staple. It was old school: clams oreganata, linguini Bolognese etc.

At least once each week, we would stop there with the boys after Jiu Jitsu. It was one of our calm places, where we could forget all the trouble and just laugh and eat and enjoy each other's company.

We would invariably order stuffed artichokes—one of those "experimental" dishes for the boys, which they wound up loving, for the taste or for the novelty, or for the fun of peeling them open…who cares, what's the difference. Food = Love.

METHOD

1. Pull the outside leaves off the artichokes; slice off the pointy tops of the rest so they have a flat top.
2. In a large pot add the vegetable broth, white wine, 1 Tablespoon oil, 1 clove of garlic chopped coarsely, ½ the chopped parsley and oregano. Set the 4 artichokes on a metal steamer at the bottom. Liquid can move up through the holes, but not too much over the steamer. Let them cook over medium heat for around half an hour. By a half hour, check on them and move them around a bit. I take a pair of tongs and start to push the leaves open a bit to see how tender they are. When the leaves gently pull away that is good. The bottom of the artichoke should be very tender to a fork or knife. SAVE THE LIQUID and set it aside.
3. While they are cooking, take another Tablespoon of oil and sauté the other clove of garlic (finely chopped), the rest of the oregano and parsley until fragrant. Add the breadcrumbs and few spoons of the liquid to create a coarse paste/ mealy consistency.
   Add pepper and salt to taste.
4. Preheat the oven to 400°F.
5. With the last Tablespoon of oil, coat the bottom of a square baking dish that's at least 1 inch deep. When the artichokes are done, set them in the pan. Spread the leaves out from the center, but do not pull them off. You want them open enough to stuff with the breadcrumb mixture; it is not a neat job.

6. Pour about 1 cup of reserved liquid into the bottom of the dish.
7. Bake for 10 to 15 minutes, drizzling the liquid over the breadcrumb mixture a couple of times so it doesn't get dry while it browns. When done the breadcrumb mixture should be moist and browned and even a little dark at points. Most of the liquid should have been poured over the baking artichokes and be thicker at the bottom of the pan.

I serve them hot and take the remaining gooey delicious liquid in the pan and pour it over the artichokes in the serving dish or eat with crunchy warm bread. Sooooooo good.

RICOTTA BRUSCHETTA

SERVES 4

INGREDIENTS

French baguette, sliced into half slices (I like them on the diagonal—*looks fancy*)
1 container fresh ricotta (about 2½ cups)
zest of 2 lemons (plus a squirt of lemon juice)
2 Tablespoons mild flavored honey
handful of basil leaves cut in strips
touch of salt and crushed black pepper

This is a lovely and light bruschetta which you can modify to your own taste preferences as I have, but this is all about the quality of the ricotta. If you can, please try to buy "homemade" ricotta; it really makes a difference. But, if you cannot, try to buy a whole milk version, or a full-fat vegan substitute. This is not a very precise recipe so you can adjust the amount of all ingredients you use per your taste.

METHOD

1. Cut and toast your bread in a toaster oven until slightly browned on one side, then flip to lightly brown the other. Lay it out on a serving tray/ platter/ clean wood cutting board (my choice).
2. Mix the ricotta with the lemon zest. We don't like it too lemony so taste before you add more. If the ricotta is unsalted add a bit of coarse salt.
3. Spread the ricotta on the toast and drizzle with honey (not too much) then toss some of the basil strips on top of the toasts and serve.

ROASTED ROSEMARY POTATOES

SERVES 4

INGREDIENTS

6-7 medium unpeeled Yukon Gold and red potatoes mixed, cleaned
2 Tablespoons olive oil
1 Tablespoon diced fresh rosemary, or dry if needed
1 Tablespoon crushed sage
salt and pepper, to taste
*optional: sprinkle of garlic powder with the salt and pepper (I do it)
*optional: 2 Tablespoons grated Parmigiano-Reggiano (at the end, maybe 5 minutes before you take them out of the oven—but definitely not necessary)

It feels funny for me to write down this recipe. Roasted potatoes are a window to my soul. There may be no more perfect food for me. So having to put this into words, in an actual recipe, is just bizarre because I could make them in my sleep, dreaming of fireflies…I mean, with my left hand tied and a blindfold…you get it. I just can't live without them, and really nobody should.

Ina Garten once told me—well, not me personally, but in a recipe—that I should parboil my potatoes first, and she is pretty much always right. And I have done this with a lot of potato recipes, but most of the time I am too lazy or time-pressed for that step—and they taste pretty damn good without doing that. But if you want to be all Ina perfect and great, do that with the potatoes before you roast them.

METHOD

Preheat the oven to 400°F.

1. Parboil the potatoes, about 15 minutes for small potatoes. You'll know they're done when they are fork-tender, but not falling apart.
2. When they're cool enough to touch, cut the potatoes into 1-inch pieces, toss on a baking tray—don't crowd them too much, so if you need 2 pans, just use 2 pans; they will taste better if more sides are crunchy.
3. Toss them with the olive oil (so they and the tray/s are coated), toss in the rosemary, sage, salt and pepper (I tend to emphasize pepper when I make these). If you want to add some garlic powder do it now as well.
4. Roast for about half an hour, but toss them and move them around every 10 minutes or so. You will likely need to detach some from the pan, and that's OK, just be aggressive and use a heavy metal spatula. You want them to be brown and crunchy, not burnt.
5. When they are almost done, I sometimes sprinkle with grated Parmigiano…just because life is short.

Let them sit and "rest" in the pan before you serve them, about 5–10 minutes.

I really can't picture life without them.

LAURA'S (NOW FAMOUS) GUACAMOLE

SERVES 4

INGREDIENTS

2 large ripe avocados
6 sweet cherry tomatoes, diced (substitute with pomegranate seeds: *pretty*)
1 Tablespoon olive oil
1 large clove garlic, crushed
½ medium shallot, finely chopped
1 Tablespoon fresh cilantro, finely chopped
1 squeeze fresh lime juice
1 teaspoon finely chopped jalapeño (powder)
½ teaspoon red pepper flakes
1 teaspoon finely chopped poblano pepper
2¼ teaspoons cayenne pepper (powder)
1 teaspoon hot Mexican green pepper hot sauce (if you can find it, also can substitute with other non-Asian hot sauce)

Harley definitely loves my guac. The rest of my family loves it too. AND …not only are my nearest and dearest all fans, but my guac was outed publicly by Steve Zing, Arthur Rizk and Joe Affe, on video…for the world to see!

It is pretty damn good and so easy. But it requires love. The kind of love that adds no less than three types of chiles and sometimes four. You can be creative with your mix of chiles but definitely have jalapeño—powdered or fresh—and crushed red in the mix.

NOTE: I know some people hate cilantro. I don't understand it, but I am no food tyrant…feel free to make this without cilantro. And on one occasion I even substituted it with fresh basil, which was surprisingly pleasant—different, yes, but very tasty. You do you!

METHOD

1. Peel the avocados and add to a large mixing bowl. Retain 1 pit and set aside. Smash the avocado with a fork. Add the olive oil and smash some more.
2. Chop the cherry tomatoes, diced very small. Add all, including the liquid, to the guacamole.
3. Salt and crushed black pepper to taste.

Alternatively: You can use pomegranate seeds to replace the sweetness of the tomatoes and it adds its own unique flavor and looks beautiful!

4. Add all remaining ingredients into the bowl and mix.

Mix everything to your preferred chunky or creamy texture.

NOTE: this is NOT a precise science. We are not making a soufflé; the fact is you can add it all in any order you want…it will taste the same in the end ;) And play with the amount of heat, lime, etc. so it works for you. This is now YOUR guacamole recipe.

Steve Zing, Arthur Rizk, Joe Affe

MY MOM'S OUTSTANDING CAPONATA

SERVES MANY

This is the SHIZ. Normally traditional caponata is a bit too olive-y for me. I LOVE olives, don't get me wrong, but normal caponata seems to always be prepared with a little too much intensity for my taste. Somehow, my mother has transformed this dish into something sublime. I am delighted to share this treat with you.

INGREDIENTS

1 large eggplant (1¼–1½ pounds halved lengthwise and cut into ½-inch pieces)
Salt to taste
3–4 Tablespoons extra virgin olive oil, as needed
2 large garlic cloves, minced
1½ pounds tomatoes (my mom uses cherry tomatoes and does not peel them)
1 teaspoon sugar or agave
Fresh ground pepper, to taste
2 Tablespoons pomegranate molasses
2–3 Tablespoons Italian parsley, chopped
⅔ cup sliced, pitted green olives (Cerignola if possible)

METHOD

Preheat the oven to 450°F.

1. Lightly coat a nonstick baking pan with olive oil. Lay the eggplant slices on top. Salt lightly and brush with olive oil. Bake for 20 minutes until the eggplant is slightly browned and soft to the touch (the surface will be dry). Cover with foil and allow the eggplant to soften and steam a bit inside the foil while you prepare the rest.
2. Heat 2 Tablespoons olive oil over medium heat in a large heavy-lidded Dutch oven or frying pan. Add the minced garlic. Cook just until fragrant, about 30 seconds.
3. Stir in the chopped tomatoes, salt to taste (½ teaspoon) and the sugar (½ teaspoon) and pepper, to taste. Bring to a simmer, and simmer uncovered over medium heat for 10 to 15 minutes, stirring often, until the tomatoes have cooked down and smell very fragrant.
4. Add the eggplant, molasses, and olives. Cover and simmer for another 20–30 minutes, stirring from time to time. The mixture should be thick, and the eggplant should be very tender, melting into the mixture. Taste, and adjust seasoning.

Allow to cool to warm or room temperature, sprinkle with chopped parsley and serve.

*My mom serves with various breads, focaccia, and crackers.

POTATO PANCAKES

SERVES 4–6

INGREDIENTS

3 pounds russet potatoes, peeled
1 cup yellow onions, quartered
3 eggs, or egg substitute
½ cup all-purpose flour
1 teaspoon baking powder
1 Tablespoon fresh Italian parsley, chopped
1 teaspoon salt
ground pepper, to taste
peanut (or other good frying oil) for pan

I love all things potato, as I have mentioned. Potato pancakes are perfect in so many ways—not least of all because they are made of potatoes and then fried! My recipe is kind of a mash-up between the traditional potato pancake and a latke. So call these whatever you want; you'll be sure to enjoy them.

METHOD

Preheat the oven to 250°F.

1. Once the potatoes are peeled, let them sit in ice cold water for at least 10 minutes while you gather the other items to prepare the pancakes.
2. Insert the medium shredding blade to a food processor. The shredding can be done with a traditional box grater, but will take some time and likely some knuckle, ouch...just make sure they look like this.
3. Shred both the potatoes and onions.
4. Once shredded, set the mixture on paper towels (or clean dish towels) and cover and pat to dry completely. You want to squeeze out most of the liquid.
5. In a large mixing bowl combine the eggs, flour, baking powder, parsley with the potato-onion combo.
6. In a large frying pan heat ⅛" peanut oil (or other frying oil). Take a small piece of the mix and place it in the oil—if it starts frying you are ready to go; if not, give it a few more minutes. Using a ⅓ cup measure, pour a scoop of the potato mixture in the pan and flatten with a wooden spatula. Fry until crisp, then flip to fry the other side until equally brown and crunchy, about 3–4 minutes per side. Cook them one at a time, with love.
7. As you complete each pancake, remove from the oil and set on paper towels or a clean dish towel to drain. Then keep warm in the oven until they are all done and ready to serve.

Lots of people serve them with sour cream or applesauce. I am a purist and just like them naked. Do whatever you prefer and enjoy them however you want.

Note: I know my tastes are sometimes a little odd, but I could eat these, my German cucumber salad, and a glass of crisp Riesling and call it a perfect day! I know it's not the most nutritious meal, but *sometimes you gotta do what you gotta do*. And I always recall the critical words of my insanely fit mother, which she told me at a very young and impressionable age: "Your body gets accustomed to itself, and eating outrageous junk one day will not change anything—your body won't know what to do with it...so just move on and don't beat yourself up." Love.

ONION BHAJI

SERVES 4–6

INGREDIENTS

2 Tablespoons chickpea flour
peanut, or other good oil for frying
2 medium red onions, sliced
1 teaspoon ground turmeric
1 teaspoon ground cumin
1 teaspoon garam masala
salt and ground pepper, to taste
water

Rumor has it these were invented for the Brits. Kind of like when Chinese food swept America in the 1950s and those intrepid restaurants had to cater to our American tastebuds, I was somehow informed that these little gems were similarly created to cater to the Brits' love for Indian food—as long as it caters to their "unique" tastebuds, LOL. Regardless of the history, they rock…you're welcome.

NOTE: I often use a smaller pan when frying; it may take longer but I waste less oil. I also try to re-use frying oil because I do not fry meat or fish.

METHOD

1. Mix the flour, about ½ teaspoon salt, pepper and spices together and add ¾ cup water. Mix the batter; it should be thick but workable. Add more water if needed. Stir in the onions so they are completely coated.
2. In a frying pan, add peanut oil so there is about 1½" in the pan.
3. Heat the oil, and wait patiently. Try dropping a little bit in the oil which should fry furiously when ready. Once the oil is ready, drop heaping Tablespoonfuls of the batter into the hot oil. They should float. Don't crowd them. Cook for a few minutes, watching them and turning them at least once until they are evenly browned. Remove when done and drain on paper towel or clean dishtowel.

Cook the remainder until done.

Serve hot with raita (recipe on page 146).

LUCIANA'S TRIFOLATA

SERVES 4–6

INGREDIENTS

6 small zucchini
salt and ground pepper
1 large clove garlic, diced fine
2 Tablespoons light olive oil
¼ cup fresh Italian parsley, chopped
½ cup Parmigiano, or substitute, grated

There are few people in my life that I recall with more fondness and love than Luciana Pisa Gheda, and the many things she taught me, and the gestures of love and kindness she showed me. I keep them with me every day of my life. She was a second mother to me, when I really needed one.

Among the wonderful life skills and charming domestic habits that she taught me, she also showed me how to make some very beautiful food. Her "trifolata" is one of those dishes, which will always conjure deep summer on Lake Garda in northern Italy. It will always take me to their little "Orto" behind the house bursting with green beans, zucchini, and tomatoes, next to a sweet little cutting garden for flowers to display all summer long. Good Lord, I can smell the fragrance rising from the garden in the late afternoon—vegetables bursting with ripeness and begging to be picked; luscious, visceral, unforgettable.

I am not sure that I have ever experienced zucchini that tasted so good ever since. But farmers in my area, and friends with gardens, do a pretty good job. The key here: keep them small. The smaller the squash, the more intense the flavor—don't let them get too big or they taste like nothing (*sa di niente*). If you can find fresh, local little zucchini for this dish you will win.

METHOD

1. Slice zucchini in ¼" rounds and place in a colander tossed with about 1 teaspoon of salt; allow to rest for about 5–10 minutes. You may want to place the colander in the sink or over a bowl as lots of water will drain out.
2. In a frying pan add oil and fry the garlic for about 30 seconds, then add the chopped parsley; do not brown the garlic, so watch it and let it cook for about 2 minutes moving it around with the parsley.
3. Add the zucchini. Add pepper (I grind about 7 times). You might add a little more salt. Either way, cook in its own liquid that it will keep producing as it cooks down.

Keep moving the contents around as they soften and blend together like a chunky purée.

Turn off the heat, add cheese and mix well.

Serve warm or at room temperature.

ROASTED BUTTERNUT SQUASH

SERVES 4

INGREDIENTS

1 medium butternut squash, peeled and chopped into 1-inch square/triangular pieces
¼ cup dark brown sugar
salt and a healthy dose of ground black pepper
2 Tablespoons light olive oil

MY CUTTING METHOD

I like to first rinse it off and dry it so it doesn't slide around. I lay the pup on its side, and cut 1-inch rounds. You should be able to cut 3–4 of these until you hit the bulbous part at the bottom. That is the challenging bit because all the seeds are in there. I usually leave that part till the end and do my best to get a few weird-shaped pieces out of it. I also usually save the seeds to toast later (I LOVE THEM—they are, along with acorn squash seeds, better tasting and more tender than pumpkin seeds).

I cut the skin off the rounds first and then cut the pieces into square-ish triangles.

This was a surprisingly lovely recipe I learned from a friend in Sacramento years ago. I learned it alongside these insane bacon-date-almond things. I may be the first person to mention bacon in a vegetarian cookbook, but there…I did it. I don't eat those anymore, but MAN were they delish! I will save those for another book ;)

Sorry for the bacon distraction—let's get back to these morsels of savory-sweet-deliciousness.

METHOD

Heat the oven to 450°F.

1. Thinly coat a large baking pan (with a lip) with olive oil.

I know that peeling butternut squash is a pain in the ass. But I wouldn't have you do it if it wasn't worth it. The best advice I can offer is to use a really good quality sharp paring knife—and BE CAREFUL.

2. Once you have your cut squash, place the pieces in a mixing bowl and add oil and sugar, salt, and start grinding that pepper…put more pepper than you think is normal. The pepper really works beautifully with the sweet caramelized squash and brown sugar.
3. Lay these pieces out on the baking pan so they do not touch each other. This allows for even browning.
4. Place the pan in the oven and check on the pieces in about 10–15 minutes. They should be ready for the first flip. I do this with tongs instead of a spatula because I don't want them rubbing up against each other and mangling my caramelizing ritual. If you don't have the time for that kind of fastidious bullshit, just flip 'em.

All in all, they take about 40 minutes in the oven, but BEWARE—the last 10 minutes they can burn. The sugar hits a certain place and then, like nuts in a pan, they are burnt when you turn your back to grab a paper towel.

So watch, flip but don't get neurotic for the first half hour, then stay close and check them. Feel free to keep flipping for maximum ass-painery.

This is a great dish in fall, as a side to any number of dishes, from Indian to Chinese to flatbread—the flavors are distinct but complementary.

SUMMER BORLOTTI BEANS

SERVES 2 FOR A MAIN COURSE, 4 AS A SIDE

INGREDIENTS

- 2 pounds borlotti beans (cranberry beans) in the pod
- 1 large shallot, sliced into long incredibly fine slivers
- 1 Tablespoon salt
- 3 Tablespoons extra virgin olive oil
- 1 Tablespoon balsamic vinegar (for cooking, not too dense)

I never ate borlotti beans until one summer in Italy on Lake Garda in my early twenties. I had never heard of them, and honestly beans were not big in my home.

In the small "fruttivendolo" (fruit and vegetable store) in Polpenazze del Garda, the tiny 15th-century town at the top of the hill, all the summer fruit and vegetables were set out in baskets, and these wonderful white- and red-speckled bean stalks were in abundance. In the U.S. they are called cranberry beans and recently I have been lucky enough to find them near me.

You can also buy them dry, and when I feel a deep need for them I will use the dry ones in soup, for example, but there is nothing so wonderful as fresh. In fact, visually, opening the pod and seeing the variations of pink and white striations and specks and dots is magical in and of itself; it is "summer" for me.

This is one of those dishes that is best appreciated using the fresh beans.

METHOD

1. Heat a medium pot, relatively full of water (at least 2" between water and top of pan), until it boils. While it is heating add 1 Tablespoon olive oil and all the salt.
2. While the water is heating, shell your beautiful beans. You will get mostly speckled ones but every so often a very pink one will make an appearance.
3. Rinse your shelled beans, and once the water is boiling, drop the beans in the water. Stir occasionally.
4. Slice your shallots sliver-thin and place the slices in a small bowl of cold water. Let them soak while you wait for the beans to cook.
5. Check the tenderness after about 10 minutes at a medium-low boil. They should still be pretty hard, then check again after another 10 minutes and so on until they are tender and soft, but not mush. You do not want the skin of the bean to completely fall apart.

6. When they are done, quickly strain and rinse with cold water so they stop cooking. The salt will have gotten inside while cooking, but after the rinse you may need to add a little more salt, your choice; taste one.
7. Once the beans have cooled and are pretty dry and free from excess water, pour into a serving bowl and toss with the rest of the olive oil, vinegar and shallot slivers (removed from the water).

Mix well and check once again for salt and serve. So lovely.

WILD MUSHROOM AND ARUGULA FLATBREAD

SERVES 4

INGREDIENTS

4 cups of wild mushrooms
(like shiitake, oyster, or porcini)
5 to 6 pieces dried porcini mushrooms
(reconstituted in ⅓ cup warm water, about 15-20 minutes until soft and pliable, reserve the water)
2 small shallots, chopped
2 Tablespoons olive oil
2 cups of organic baby arugula, chopped to 1-inch pieces
2–3 Tablespoons Parmigiano Reggiano or substitute (nutritional yeast)
Salt and pepper to taste
2 frozen rectangular flatbread crusts, or package of naan (2 pieces), or 2 round pita (if you can't find the naan). You can also use pizza crust, chickpea, or cauliflower variations as well.

Arugula Dressing

1 Tablespoon olive oil
½ Tablespoon champagne vinegar
(or other good white wine vinegar)
salt and pepper

We love flatbreads. They are less heavy than a pizza and more useful as a conduit of toppings that you might not want on an entire pizza. I serve them as a side dish as well as hors d'oeuvres. For this recipe I prefer to use ones that are rectangular and long, they seem to work better than naan—but it's really up to you. I like the little rectangles I serve; they look good, and that matters too!

*__NOTE__: If you are using a frozen bread, I generally just sprinkle a little bit of water on the side that will touch the pan and then set the pieces directly on the hot pan so they do not stick. I recommend freezing the bread you use first. If you are concerned about it sticking, add a little olive oil to the pan with a paper towel or spray with olive oil baking/cooking spray. For naan and pita I also heat on one side first, then flip it and add the mushroom mixture, so it becomes evenly crunchy.

**I also frequently make this flatbread without the arugula and it is fantastic as well.

METHOD

1. Preheat oven to 400°F.
2. Clean and chop mushrooms to about 1-inch-long pieces. This is not a science; I just don't like mushrooms that are too big or long or dangly that they pull off the bread when you bite down—*and drip oil onto your shirt*. Take the porcini out of the water and reserve the water. Chop the porcini quite small—they are powerful and you want them spread around.
3. In a heavy pan, heat oil at medium heat, add shallots and stir; cook until translucent (about 3 minutes). Add the rehydrated porcini.
4. After another minute or so, add the other mushrooms and sauté on medium heat, moving them around in the pan frequently until browned and tender (about 15 minutes).
5. Add salt and pepper (I tend to go a bit heavier on the pepper here as I think pepper complements mushrooms really well). Continue to mix. They should be uniformly browned and some even getting crispy.
6. Add the retained porcini mushroom water, pouring it back into the pan through a paper towel (to sift out any particles). Cook down the water, stirring constantly.
7. At this stage you can toss about a tablespoon of Parmigiano Reggiano or substitute (like nutritional yeast) in the mushrooms and mix. The mixture will now become creamy. Set the mushrooms aside.

Place your baking sheet in the oven so it gets hot.

8. In a large bowl place the chopped arugula and sprinkle with the dressing ingredients. The leaves should just be coated. You don't want the arugula heavily dressed.
9. Pull the baking sheet out of the oven, lay out the two rectangular flatbread pieces (or whatever bread you are using) on the baking sheet, spread a little more cheese or nutritional yeast on the bread—then top evenly with the mushroom mixture and return to the oven for about 15–20 minutes. Check on it as you don't want the bread to burn, and it is good to make sure the bread isn't sticking to the pan.
10. It should come out of the oven a bit browned on the edges. I place the pieces on a clean, dry cutting board and sprinkle with the chopped arugula. Then cut in small rectangles or triangles with a pizza cutter and serve.

*You could add some grated cheese, but I think the flavors are beautifully complementary without the addition of any more cheese.

CRUNCHY CAULIFLOWER WITH CAPERS

SERVES 4

INGREDIENTS

1 medium cauliflower
2 medium shallots, chopped fine
1 clove garlic, minced
2 Tablespoons light olive oil
1 Tablespoon capers (in brine, *not* salted or in balsamic)
½ cup plain breadcrumbs
1 Tablespoon chopped fresh parsley
½ cup Parmigiano Reggiano or nutritional yeast (I usually use nutritional yeast)
salt and pepper, to taste

Cauliflower has long been a misunderstood vegetable. I think its humble looks and unglamorous reputation have sapped this wonderful food of its full culinary potential. Cauliflower needs better PR—maybe an agent. It is versatile and dynamic and is simply underpraised for all it does and can do. Nothing competes with potatoes for me, but cauliflower is a close contender.

I use cauliflower in an endless number of dishes, from all parts of the world, and what I think is most cool about it is that I can experiment, and I do regularly. Cauliflower is one of those vegetables that for both texture and taste, and the way it cooks down or stays crunchy, can do many unexpected and experimental things, and I like that.

METHOD

1. Heat oven to 400°F.
2. Clean cauliflower and remove the green parts and the "core" by cutting it in half and then make a triangle cut in the stalk to cut out the toughest part.

I wash all the pieces and save the parts I am not cooking with for vegetable stock in the freezer.

3. Chop up the cauliflower and don't get crazy like I often do and focus on making tiny little perfect trees like an OCD freak. Just chop chop chop chop until you have crumbles.
4. Add 1 Tablespoon of the olive oil to a baking pan.
5. Toss all cauliflower into the pan. Add the shallots, parsley, breadcrumbs, capers, salt and pepper. With your hands mix this all up really well along with the rest of the olive oil.
6. Place the tray in the oven and roast for about 20 minutes. Then toss and mix it all in the pan. Return to the oven. It should be starting to brown very nicely. After another 10 minutes, add the grated Parmigiano-Reggiano or nutritional yeast and toss it all very well. Let it cook for another 10 minutes after adding the cheese and check it, so it doesn't burn. Add more salt/pepper if needed.

It should all be browned, crispy and crunchy.

You can serve it hot or warm—either way it is delightful.

PESTO STUFFED MUSHROOMS

SERVES 10–15

INGREDIENTS

30–40 white mushrooms (not too big, not too small)
1 cup pesto (homemade [see page 36] is always preferred but not necessary)
¼ cup Parmigiano Reggiano or substitute
1 egg, or egg substitute
½ cup panko or other breadcrumbs
1 large clove garlic, minced
1 Tablespoon light olive oil

My mom has been making these little wonders for as long as I can remember. At this point I can't recall if they were her invention or my grandmother's. When I was applying to law school my essay was about why copyright law should change to permit the copyright of recipes, and I used this one as my example and included it with the essay. I'm a dork down deep (or not so deep).

These are so easy and so delicious they will become a go-to for you as well.

METHOD

1. Heat the oven to 350°F.
2. Clean off your mushrooms and pull out the stems. Take a couple of handfuls of the stems and dice them—not more than a cup. Set them aside.
3. In a frying pan, add olive oil and minced garlic. Sauté for a couple of minutes until the garlic just starts to brown, add the chopped mushroom stems and mix together for a minute. Turn the heat off and add the egg and stir well. The egg will turn opaque but not really cook. It is really a binder more than anything else.
4. Add the pesto, breadcrumbs, and mix it all. I like to add some ground pepper. The pesto already has salt, so no need to add more, unless you want to. The consistency should be moist but very chunky.
5. Scoop the mixture into the mushroom caps until you have a nice plump, round dome of tightly packed stuffing.
6. In a baking dish, preferably with a rack, carefully place each mushroom cap—do not let them touch each other! They hate each other and must be kept separated! LOL. Bake them for about 25–30 minutes and check on them after 20. They should be starting to get toasted and brown on the top when you take them out.

*Since their less-than-glamorous appearance belies their fabulous deliciousness, my mother, who is generally better than me, takes little pieces of mozzarella and places them on the top of each dome to melt into snowy-white, charming little tops, and bakes for a couple more minutes. As I said, I am not as good as her and rarely take this extra step...but please, go for it (*show-off*)!

JEANNE'S KNÆKBRØD

MAKES ABOUT 20 CRACKERS

INGREDIENTS

1½ cups rye flour
¼ cup steel-cut oats
¼ cup sesame seeds
¼ cup sunflower seeds, shucked
¼ cup pumpkin seeds
¼ cup flaxseed
1 Tablespoon baking powder
½ teaspoon salt
⅔ cup light olive oil
⅔ cup water

Harley has an extraordinary family in Denmark. He arrived in Aarhus as a three-year-old child and stayed—with trips back and forth to New York—until he was 12. He was a truly bicultural child and some of his most formative memories were made in Aarhus; and thank God for that, because the Stateside "lifestyle" needed that balance, or he probably would not have survived.

Jeanne is Harley's stepmom, and one of the most wonderful people I have ever had the pleasure of having in my life and in my family. And not only is she a wonderful human, she is also a wonderful cook, who has shared one of the most delicious and traditionally Scandinavian recipes with me...and which I am now sharing with all of you lucky foodies ☺

METHOD

1. Preheat oven to 300°F.
2. Mix all ingredients and knead into a dough. It will be soft and moist and stick incessantly to your hands. Divide the dough into 2 parts.
3. In the pan, roll the dough thin (about ⅛ inch) between 2 pieces of wax paper. Cut the dough into 9 rectangles.
4. Leave the rolled dough, cut into rectangles on the parchment paper, on the baking sheet and place in the preheated oven. Bake approximately 20–25 minutes at 300°F. You can turn the sheet as it goes. Check on it every 15 minutes. The dough should be hard and starting to brown when done.

Remove the pan from the oven and let them cool on the pan for about 10 minutes before moving them to cooling rack. I then roll the other ball of dough and make the second group of crackers.

They are so delicious plain, and then add some cheese or nut butter or whatever you choose, and it is another level. They are healthy and filling and pretty much the perfect snack!

CUCUMBER GINGER RAITA

INGREDIENTS

1 medium English cucumber (or 3 small Persians)
1 teaspoon ground cumin
1 teaspoon ground coriander
1 teaspoon minced fresh ginger
2 cups plain Greek yogurt or cashew yogurt
½ teaspoon ground red chile pepper
1 Tablespoon chopped fresh cilantro (optional if you hate it)
salt and ground pepper, to taste

METHOD

Wash the cucumber and coarsely chop. Add it to a Cuisinart or blender with all the other ingredients and pulse. You can decide how chunky you like it—I like it smooth and creamy, so I blend for a little while. I leave the skin on because I love the sea-foam color it becomes.

BABA GHANOUSH

INGREDIENTS

1 large eggplant or 2 small to medium Italian eggplants (about 1 pound)
1 medium clove of garlic, pressed or minced
1 Tablespoon lemon juice, more if necessary
3 Tablespoons fruity extra virgin olive oil (it will not be heated)
2 Tablespoons chopped Italian parsley
2 Tablespoons tahini
*NOTE: I can't seem to make tahini properly and I always forget to buy it. I generally just dump about 2 Tablespoons of toasted sesame seeds in the Cuisinart and it tastes great.
salt and ground pepper, to taste

METHOD

1. Heat oven to 420°F.
2. Wash the eggplant(s) and cut the top off only. Poke the skin with a fork a couple of times and set it on a baking tray in the oven. Cook for about 30–40 minutes and turn once. It is OK if it gets browned on the side sitting on the pan.
3. Pull it out with tongs and let it "rest" (love that expression) on a plate or in a shallow bowl (a bowl is often better, because when you do cut it open usually a lot of liquid pours from the cutting board onto the floor... just FYI). Give it about 15 minutes to cool.
4. I slice it down the middle and try to retain the liquid as best I can. The skin will peel off easily. I generally hold the half of eggplant over the Cuisinart and peel the skin away. All of the soft part—with no skin—should go in the food processor bowl. If there is liquid in the plate, I pour that in the bowl as well.
5. Add all other ingredients and blend. Then pulse until you get the consistency you want. People like it different ways—we like baba ghanoush super creamy—so add more olive oil if needed.

Serve warm or at room temperature.

sweets

Kheer
Apple Crisp
Peach Cobbler
Apple Raisin Bread
Banana Bread
Oatmeal Lace Cookies
Gingerbread Cookies
Lisa's Coconut Pie

Truth be told, I am not that into sweets. I don't love chocolate or ice cream or dessert. I know…it's a disorder, but it's been my disorder from birth, so I am used to it. I am also used to getting worlds of shit about it too. But I do like to make sweets. My mom is an amazing baker. She makes the most beautiful cookies and cakes, even perfect soufflé! I tend to gravitate to salty and savory, and so that has left my baking in the super simple, easy department. It all tastes delish, but it is stupid simple, no fuss, warm-and-fuzzy basic yum.

These are some of the standards in regular rotation at the Flanagan house. And P.S., aside from the kheer, you will see that everything I make *should* be enjoyed with ice cream. Harley is pretty serious about ice cream, and since we have been limiting dairy, we found some amazing brands of non-dairy ice cream. Harley's faves:

> **So Delicious** *Salted Caramel* and *Snickerdoodle* and **Oatly** *Coffee* or *Vanilla* are particularly delicious with the desserts here.

KHEER

SERVES ABOUT 8

INGREDIENTS

2 cups coconut milk (I use organic)
2 cups whole milk or creamy almond milk
3 Tablespoons honey
1½ cup basmati rice
½ teaspoon ground cardamom
¼ teaspoon salt
¼ cup sliced toasted almonds (optional)

The first time I had kheer was at an Indian restaurant on East 6th Street, when East 6th Street was all-Indian-all-the-time. I remember it so well because it was the 4th of July and shortly after dinner there was a miserable failed attempt to watch the fireworks on 14th Street near the ConEd plant. It was an epic fail evening, but not the kheer—that blew my mind with its delicate, creamy richness. After finding this wonderful dish I was even able to eat regular rice pudding…but it does not really compare. Of the many attempts I have made, modifications and experimentation, this recipe is the one we like the best:

METHOD

1. Combine the milks and the honey in a medium saucepan and bring to a boil. Add the rice and lower the heat. Simmer and keep stirring as the liquid thickens and the rice cooks. This will take about 15–20 minutes.
2. Stir in the cardamom. Cook and stir a few more minutes; turn off the heat.
3. I transfer the pudding to small serving bowls on a tray and let them cool in the refrigerate until they "set." You can sprinkle the almonds on top when you serve.

APPLE CRISP

SERVES 4–6

INGREDIENTS

4 cups cubed, peeled apples (about 4 medium)—I use Granny Smiths
⅔ cup dark brown sugar
½ cup organic flour (I like chickpea or oat flour, but use all-purpose for a more traditional taste)
½ cup rolled oats
¾ teaspoon ground cinnamon
¾ teaspoon ground nutmeg
¾ teaspoon ground cloves
¾ cup softened butter or vegan butter substitute

This is simple classic, feel-good, Americana dessert in my opinion. Apples cook so wonderfully and they combine deliciously with the buttery crunchy crumbles. Add a little ice cream and I don't know why you need anything more complicated.

METHOD

1. Preheat the oven to 350°F.
2. Grease a nonstick bread pan. Spread the apple pieces evenly in the pan.
3. Mix the other ingredients together and then lay the mixture over the apples.
4. Bake for about 30–40 minutes until the apples are tender and bubbly and crumbly topping becomes browned.

Serve with ice cream or non-dairy version.

PEACH COBBLER

SERVES 4–6

INGREDIENTS

Filling

8–10 fresh peaches
*enough for 5 cups peeled and sliced
¼ cup dark brown sugar
1 teaspoon cinnamon
1 Tablespoon vanilla extract
2 Tablespoons corn starch

Topping

1½ cups flour (I like chickpea or oat, but all-purpose flour is perfect)
1½ teaspoons baking powder
1 teaspoon cinnamon
½ teaspoon allspice
¼ cup + 2 Tablespoons dark brown sugar, divided
1 teaspoon vanilla extract
¼ cup coconut oil, melted
⅔ cup almond milk

Another Americana classic: peach cobbler, a close cousin to apple crisp—but different enough to warrant its own place in this book. When peaches are in season, to me, there is nothing more summer-licious, in every form. I am happy to literally eat them while standing over the sink and letting the peach just be a peach. This dish is vegan.

TIP: You can blanch the peaches to peel them easily. Place the whole peaches in boiling water for 1 minute. Remove and let them cool. Once they are cool enough to handle the skin will peel right off.

METHOD

1. Preheat the oven to 400°F.
2. Grease a 9×9-inch baking dish.
3. Slice the peaches and mix them together with ¼ cup of the dark brown sugar, cinnamon, vanilla and corn starch. Lay the mixture in the baking dish.
4. For the topping: mix the flour, baking powder, cinnamon, allspice and the dark brown sugar. Mix in the vanilla, coconut oil, and almond milk until all combined.
5. Scoop the topping mix over the peach filling in the baking dish. You can sprinkle the extra 2 Tablespoons of dark sugar on top if desired.
6. Bake for about 25 minutes until golden brown and the filling is bubbling. Make sure to check on it along the way so it does not burn; my oven runs hot and sometimes it happens.

Definitely serve with some sort of ice cream, frozen yogurt or frozen non-dairy something!

APPLE RAISIN BREAD

SERVES ABOUT 5

INGREDIENTS

3 cups chopped tart unpeeled apples
3 cups all-purpose flour
2½ cups dark brown sugar
1 cup vegetable oil (coconut or other mild vegetable oil)
4 eggs, beaten (I always substitute eggs with egg replacer, and it works perfectly)
1 Tablespoon vanilla extract
2 teaspoons ground cinnamon
1½ teaspoons salt
1½ teaspoons baking soda
1 teaspoon ground cloves
½ teaspoon baking powder
⅔ cup raisins
½ cup chopped walnuts (if desired)

This is it, friends: THE most delicious apple bread you will have. Period. I have been making this bread since I was a teenager and without fail it remains the best, coziest, warm-wintery bread I make. So please make it and enjoy.

METHOD

1. Preheat oven to 325°F.
2. Grease two 9×5×3 bread pans.
3. Beat all ingredients together, scraping the bowl constantly.
4. Once the mixture is smooth, pour it into the 2 pans. They should be filled to about half full (they will expand and rise as they bake).
5. Bake for about an hour. A toothpick stuck in the center should come out smooth with no batter sticking to it. Again, check your oven because if it runs hot like mine, it may bake faster.

You will love this. I serve with ice cream or non-dairy ice cream in a bowl with the bread cut in half. It is really similar to a traditional English "pudding."

THE BEST BANANA BREAD

SERVES ABOUT 5

INGREDIENTS

2 teaspoons lemon juice
(fresh or from a bottle)
⅔ cup milk or creamy almond milk
2⅓ cups all-purpose flour
(or chickpea/oat)
⅔ cups granulated turbinado sugar
1 teaspoon baking soda
1 teaspoon salt
⅔ cup neutral unflavored vegetable oil
(coconut, for example)
2 large eggs
(or equivalent egg substitute)
1⅔ cups mashed ripe bananas

Optional:
½ cup chopped walnuts

I have tried many banana bread recipes and this one is by far my favorite.

METHOD

1. Preheat the oven to 350°F.
2. Grease a 9×5×3 bread pan.
3. Mix the sugar, baking soda, flour and salt in a bowl.
4. Separately, mix the lemon juice, milk, eggs (or substitute) oil and bananas until blended and mashed up well.
5. Mix the 2 bowls of ingredients together. The consistency should be thick but still pourable.

*Add the nuts if you want them.

6. Pour the batter into a baking dish; it should come to about halfway up the pan.
7. Bake for 1 hour. Check after 45 minutes by inserting a toothpick. If batter still clings, return to oven and check again every 5 to 10 minutes. When the toothpick comes out clean, remove from the oven and cool on a rack.

OATMEAL LACE COOKIES

SERVES MANY

INGREDIENTS

½ cup melted salted butter
2½ cups rolled oats
1 cup brown sugar
2 teaspoons baking powder
1 egg, beaten, or substitute

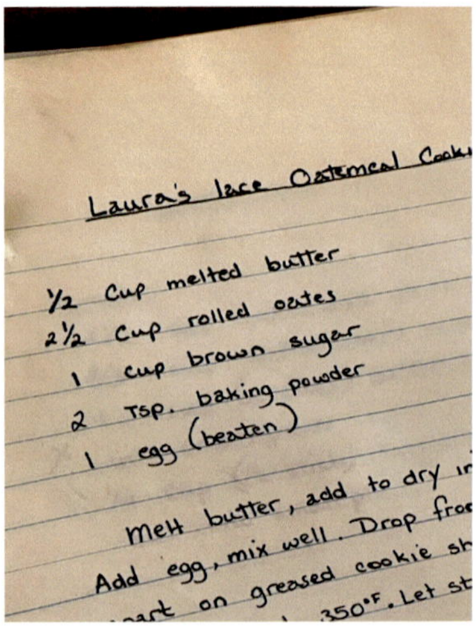

This recipe that I am about to share with you has been saved since my formative days in Mrs. Curtain's kindergarten at The Chapin School, 100 East End Avenue. As part of our holiday pageantries, I returned home with this recipe. My mom probably still has the original copy, butter stains and all.

I think the magic of these cookies, and why they went into permanent holiday rotation, is not their oatmealiness, but rather their super delicate, crunchy, snowflake-like ways. Butter or butter substitute is the star of this show, with dark brown sugar playing a critical supporting role.

*__NOTE__: they are fragile, and will often break—that is OK, because guess what, you can use the broken bits of deliciousness as crumble to throw on top of ice cream. It's so good, you might want to just smash them up and do that anyway ☺

METHOD

1. Preheat oven to 350°F.
2. Prepare a baking sheet, either greased, parchment paper or silicone sheet.
3. Add the oats, sugar and baking powder to a medium bowl and mix.
4. Add the melted butter to the dry ingredients and mix. Then add the egg. Mix it all well into a thick mush.
5. Drop spoonful dollops onto the greased baking sheet. Give them 2" space between each other because they spread.
6. Bake for 8–10 minutes. They "melt" and become quite flat and lacy-looking and crispy.
7. Remove from the oven, but let them cool in the pan for about 2 minutes.

*Carefully use a spatula to move them to a cooling rack. This is where most of the breakage will occur. Remember, it's OK...crumbles for your ice cream.

GINGERBREAD COOKIES

SERVES 10–15

Gingerbread is a favorite of mine. As someone who does not love sweets, it has a spice that distracts me from the sweetness. I like cookies as well as just plain gingerbread. I guess I'm a fan of ginger, generally. It translates from savory to sweet so well, even pickled.

I mentioned before that my mom is a crazy-good baker. When she was at the height of her holiday cookie madness some years ago, when we would all get beautiful boxes of at least five to seven different varieties at a time, she would always make a gingerbread "human" (I am being PC). One year I asked her to make gingerbread girls with my school uniform, which was a green plaid skirt. She indulged me…with the caveat that I was a rotten child and she would never do it again. I think she took it as a dare and couldn't resist the challenge. My mom is the best mom ☺

INGREDIENTS

- 1 package of vegan cook-and-serve vanilla pudding
- 1 stick salted butter, softened
- ½ cup brown sugar, firmly packed
- 1 Tablespoon honey
- 1 egg, or equivalent egg substitute
- 1½ cups all-purpose flour
- ½ teaspoon baking soda
- 1½ teaspoons ground ginger
- 1 teaspoon cinnamon
- 2 Tablespoons unsulfured molasses

Simple Cookie Frosting

- 2 cups powdered sugar
- 1½ teaspoons light corn syrup
- 2 Tablespoons milk, more as needed
- ½ teaspoon vanilla or almond extract
- food coloring, optional

METHOD

1. Preheat oven to 350°F.
2. Mix butter, sugar and pudding mix together.
3. Add egg and mix well.
4. In a separate bowl, mix flour and baking soda, ginger and cinnamon. Add to pudding mixture and stir until well blended.
5. Chill dough in the fridge until firm (at least 2 hours and then take it out for at least ½ hour before rolling).
6. Roll out on a floured board to about ⅛-inch thick and cut with a cookie cutter (in desired shape). Bake 10–20 minutes.

Method for frosting

Mix the sugar, corn syrup, milk and vanilla or almond extract. The mixture should be very smooth. Use more milk to get it to a consistency you want for how you are decorating your cookies. The consistency should be like toothpaste—it will dry hard.

Add food coloring if desired. Spread on the cookies or pipe on using a frosting bag. Allow them to dry before you touch the frosting.

LISA'S COCONUT PIE

SERVES 6

The fabled coconut pie...the pie I threw out before Harley could have a last taste—the pie he lamented publicly with his version of the Godfather's unmistakable lament, "*I Can't Believe You Threw Out the Co-co-nut Pie*"...Coconut Pie. It's really that good!

INGREDIENTS

Crust

½ cup (one stick) salted butter (slightly softened)
1 cup all-purpose flour
⅓ cup crushed pecans

Filling

1 (4.6-ounce) package of vegan cook-and-serve vanilla pudding (*there are the Jell-Os of the world, and then there are the numerous organic, non-GMO options available these days ... you know which one I am choosing)*
3 cups whole milk
1½ cups sweetened coconut flakes

Topping

1 (16-ounce) carton of heavy whipping cream
Powdered sugar to taste (up to ⅓ cup)
1–2 cups sweetened coconut flakes

METHOD

Crust

1. Heat the oven to 350°F.
2. Mix ingredients together well. This is a rustic crust; the ingredients should be fully integrated with a texture that allows you to press it into an ungreased 9.5-inch pie plate. It won't look smooth like a traditional dough pastry.
3. Bake for 10–12 minutes, until lightly brown and edges are set. Remove from the oven and allow to cool before filling.

Filling

1. While the crust is cooling, follow the cooking instructions on the pudding package (microwave on high for up to 8 minutes, stirring every 2 minutes until it comes to a boil).
2. Stir in the coconut flakes.
3. Pour into pie shell and allow to cool a bit (about 10–15 minutes), then refrigerate for at least 2 hours to set.

For the topping

1. Preheat the oven to 350°F.
2. Spread coconut evenly over an ungreased baking sheet. Bake for about 5 minutes; remove from oven and stir/toss coconut with a spatula. Return to oven and bake an additional 5 minutes or so, checking to make sure the coconut is browning appropriately and not burning.
3. Whip heavy whipping cream until stiff peaks form, adding powdered sugar as you go depending on how sweet you want it to be.

Remove the pie when ready to serve and top the chilled pie with the whipped cream (it should reach super fluffy, impressive, decadent heights!), add the toasted coconut, serve and enjoy.

ALMOND-HAZELNUT BISCOTTI

MAKES ABOUT 20 BISCOTTI

The most typical, traditional biscotti seem to be "biscotti di mandorla": almond biscotti. They were not as prevalent when I was a child, but now (in New York, anyway) they are omnipresent. They even sell them wrapped at Starbucks! I have always loved them because I have never had a sweet tooth, and a less sweet cookie is my speed for dessert.

I do love almonds, but I also enjoy hazelnut with a little cranberry and grapefruit zest; I think you will too.

INGREDIENTS

2 cups all-purpose flour
¼ teaspoon salt
1 teaspoon baking powder
1 cup granulated turbinado sugar
6 Tablespoons butter, or vegan butter, room temperature
2 eggs, or vegan egg replacer
zest of organic grapefruit (substitute lemon or orange if you prefer)
1½ teaspoons vanilla extract
1½ teaspoons almond extract
½ cup whole almonds, toasted and coarsely chopped
½ cup hazelnuts, toasted and coarsely chopped
¼ cup dried cranberries, coarsely chopped

METHOD

1. Preheat oven to 300°F.
2. On a parchment-lined baking sheet, toast your chopped almonds and hazelnuts together for about 15 minutes. Move them around a little as they toast. Set them aside (they will cook more in the biscotti).
3. Turn the oven up to 325°F.
4. Line a baking sheet (large enough for 2 "loaves" about 3½ inches wide and 12 inches long) with parchment paper and make sure the rack is in the center of the oven.
5. In a large mixing bowl, combine flour, salt, baking powder, and mix well.
6. In a large electric mixer or large bowl with a hand-held electric mixer, beat the eggs or egg substitute, room temperature butter or vegan butter, sugar, grapefruit zest, vanilla and almond extracts, for approximately 3 minutes until thick.
7. Add the flour mixture to the butter mixture a little bit at a time. The dough should be thick and dense, yet smooth. Add the toasted nuts and chopped dried cranberries. Mix on low until everything is coated with batter. Let the mixture rest 15–20 minutes. The mixture should be very moist and sticky, but you should still be able to roll it into a ball. If need be, you can add a little water until this consistency is reached.
8. Scrape the dough from the bowl onto the parchment-lined baking sheet. With a little cooking spray or oil on your hands, form 2 equal-sized "loaves." They should be about 3½ inches wide and 12 inches long and flat-ish. They should not touch.
9. Bake about 20–25 minutes until the dough is firm but gives a little when pressed. Remove from the oven. Let the loaves cool completely.
10. Turn the oven down to 300°F.
11. Once the loaves are room temperature, place them on a cutting board and slice widthwise at a diagonal angle in 1-inch-thick slices.
12. Arrange the cookies in rows on the baking sheet, and slice the second loaf.
13. Put the cookies back in the oven and bake for 8 minutes.
14. Pull the sheet out of the oven and gently flip each cookie. Bake for another 8 minutes or until nicely browned.

Remove from oven and let them cool on the baking sheet.

epilogue

THE LIFE-ALTERING GRILLED CHEESE

For any of you who know Harley, you know that, not very far beneath his gargoyle-ish exterior, he is a very gentle, generous and sentimental soul.

When his book *Hard-Core: Life of My Own* was on the verge of publication in the early fall of 2016, the *New York Times* ran a feature about him written by Charles Curkin.[1] I remember the interview like it was yesterday; I was home the whole time and toward the end of the interview Harley was rushing, as he normally does, to leave for Renzo Gracie Academy. And as usual, he had not eaten anything the entire day and it was around 3:30 in the afternoon, when the pain of starvation normally sets in for him.

Since my domestic instincts generally override all else that I am doing, I offered to make Harley a grilled cheese sandwich for the road, and as they continued to talk in the living room, I ran to the kitchen. I could see the intrigue on Charles' face as he watched our disarmingly domestic dance, with Harley running in and out of the kitchen to get his work stuff together. In no time the sandwich was done and neatly wrapped for the road (first paper towel, then tinfoil, so it doesn't get soggy).

We both laughed when the article came out in September and read the part about the grilled cheese. I thought, *wow, my first appearance in the* New York Times *and I am making a sandwich; good grief, so much for my visions of grandeur and world domination.* ☹

All joking aside, the subject of grilled cheese is, in fact, important. Harley's grandmother Beatrice used to make him grilled cheese sandwiches; Beatrice was perhaps the most consistently stable maternal figure in

1. "Punker Finds His Mellower Side," by Charles Curkin, *The New York Times*, September 4, 2016.

Harley's entire young life. In this context, when I say stable, I really mean consistent: always there and to whom he could always return. She was the reason so much of his archive exists—it all lived in her home during his crazy days. She was the adult human being to whom he could "go home" when he was homeless, hungry and in need of some refuge. And she remained in the house he knew when he was a child until she was no longer able to do so. Heavy stuff.

He told me that he never ate another grilled cheese sandwich after she died and certainly wouldn't let anyone make one for him at home. At some point in the first four years of our relationship, and I can't recall when it happened, he asked for one. It's funny how life unfolds.

I have become the inheritor of the grilled cheese mantle.

I was then, and continue to be, moved by this.

INGREDIENTS

2 slices of grainy bread; I usually have Vermont organic multi-grain slices or something like that
1 Tablespoon butter, or substitute
3 to 4 slices sharp aged cheddar, thinly sliced
3 to 4 Jarlsberg or Swiss, thinly sliced
1 medium or 2 big cherry tomatoes, sliced very thin (not necessary but Harley likes it)

I make the sandwich with a combination of the cheese I have on hand, which is usually some combination of cheddar and Jarlsberg, or Gruyère, aged Gouda or Swiss, but I have made it with mozzarella (smoked, which his son Jonah adores, or plain) as well as a pecorino with truffle (delicious). But whichever cheese I use, the most important ingredient is love—lots of love. If you don't have any to put into this sandwich, don't make it.

METHOD

1. Salt the tomato slices to get the water out in a bowl or on a small plate.
2. In a heavy frying pan, heat the butter on low until it melts and evenly coats the bottom of the pan. Add the bread and brown on one side (about 7 minutes). The heat should stay low to medium so it does not burn, but still long enough to melt the cheese.
3. Flip the bread and lay the cheese slices on one piece of the bread. Add the tomato slices. Sometimes I add a little pepper (I like pepper on everything). Place the other slice of bread on top of the cheese and tomato and press gently with the spatula. I usually lay a small flat pot lid on the sandwich to give it a little weight and heat from both sides.
4. Carefully flip the sandwich once the first side is browned. I also like to press the sides up against the pan to melt the cheese that peeks out from the bread. But whatever you do, try to make sure the cheese is melted and not still in sliced form.

I get the bread pretty brown before I take it out of the pan.

*NOTE: In recent months I have started to make more of an open-faced toasted cheese concoction for Harley—less buttery and filling. I simply toast one side of the bread in a toaster oven, then when I flip the bread, I add the cheese and let it toast until it melts. I add the sliced tomato at the end when I pull the bread out and usually add a little pepper and chopped fresh basil. Still made with the same amount of love.

menu suggestions

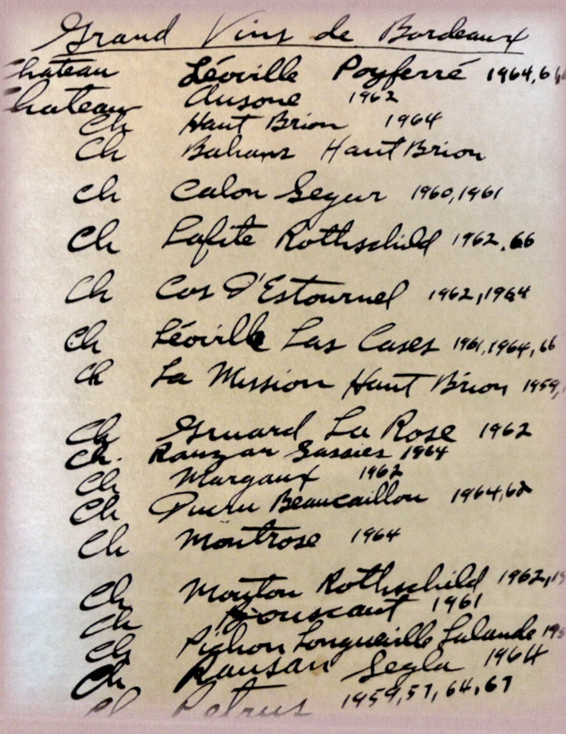

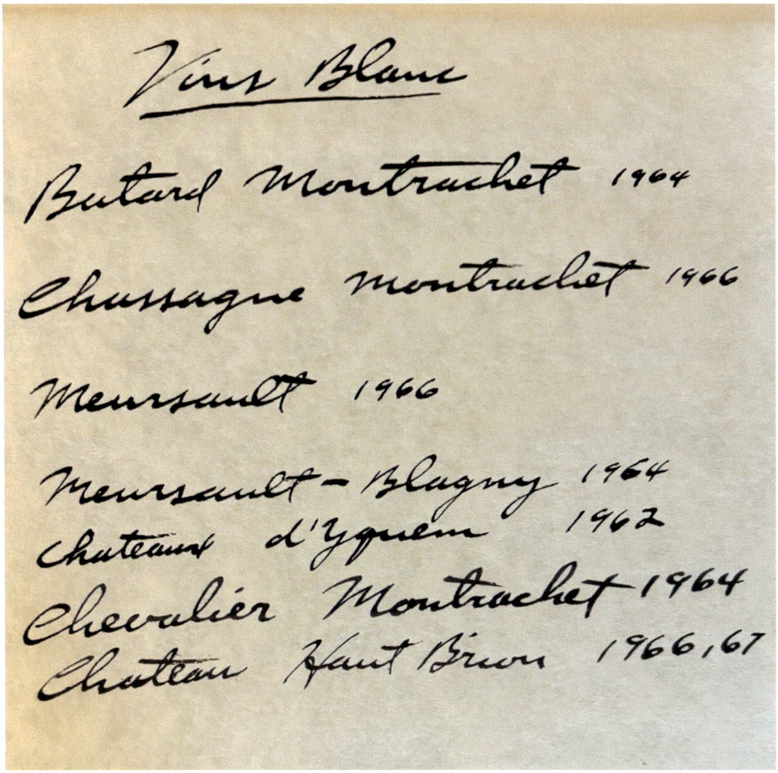

MENUS AND NOTES ON WINE

Menus

The way we eat changes over time. From many courses to small plates, dietary fads and the politics of food (factory farming, genetically modified foods, organics, etc.). We all must eat, but how we eat is indeed *a moveable feast*.

Notes on wine

My father was a wine collector. But he always said my mother had a better palate. Both were serious about wine throughout my formative years. His collection focused on French wine, but later in his life he learned more and gravitated toward Italian. My parents drank wine with dinner, and it was never taboo. They shared a more European attitude about wine: Good wine was part of the meal and was not to be had excessively. I recall having wine with dinner in my teens and continue to do so regularly to this day. I always say, *I don't have kids, so I spend my money on good wine and horses. Priorities.*

I favor Italian wine. I have had more experience with it in Italy, and understanding the language, culture, and land has enhanced my experience of the wines I love. I have selected ones that I would drink with the menus.

SEASONAL MENUS

Menus for warm days and cold nights…

Winter

1. Caesar Salad
   Vegetable Lasagna
   Biscotti
   Wine: Barolo
2. Spicy Sesame Noodles with Tofu
   Szechuan Eggplant
   Gingerbread Cookies
   Wine: Chassagne-Montrachet
3. Guacamole (+ chips)
   Veggie Burritos (with extra rice and black beans)
   Lisa's Coconut Pie
   Wine: Albariño

Summer

1. Luciana's Trifolata
   Riccioli with Homemade Pesto and Broccolini
   Summer Borlotti Beans
   Biscotti
   Wine: Lugana (Lago di Garda)
2. Crunchy Hen-of-the-Woods
   Caprese Salad
   Cacio e Pepe
   Peach Cobbler
   Wine: Sancerre
3. Baba Ghanoush
   Curried Couscous
   Simple Sautéed Spinach
   Kheer
   Wine: Côtes de Provence Rosé

Spring

1. Simple Butter Lettuce Salad
   Vegetable Fried Rice
   Soba Noodles with Miso Glazed Tofu
   Oatmeal Lace Cookies
   Wine: Riesling (dry)
2. Warm French Lentil Salad
   Pasta Primavera
   The Best Banana Bread
   Wine: Dolcetto d'Alba
3. Cucumber Salad
   Traditional Falafel and Dips
   Kheer
   Wine: Côtes de Provence Rosé

Fall

1. Guacamole (+ chips)
   Veggie Burritos (with extra rice and black beans)
   Lisa's Coconut Pie
   Wine: Rioja
2. Dal (and basmati rice)
   Massaman Curry
   Cucumber Ginger Raita (with naan)
   Kheer
   Wine: Lugana (Lago di Garda) or Riesling
3. Fennel and Parmigiano Reggiano Salad
   Roasted Romanesco Risotto
   Roasted Delicata Squash and Shallots
   Apple Raisin Bread
   Wine: Barolo

HARD HOLIDAYS FOR VEGETARIANS

When turkey, ham, or leg of lamb is the center of the meal…

NOTE: For holidays and celebrations, I always like to have olives with appetizers (also a cheese or two). With dessert I also serve nuts and fruit, depending on the season (winter: clementines and peanuts in the shell; summer: watermelon and roasted almonds).

Appetizers
- My Mom's Outstanding Caponata
- Pesto Stuffed Mushrooms
- Roasted Fennel Flatbread

Main
- Porcini Mushroom Risotto, or
- Angel Hair Mushroom Carbonara

Sides
- Simple Sautéed Spinach
- Roasted Butternut Squash

Sweets
- Gingerbread Cookies
- Oatmeal Lace Cookies
- Biscotti

Wine: Brunello di Montalcino

Appetizers
- Ricotta Bruschetta
- Wild Mushroom and Arugula Flatbread

Main
- Vegetable Lasagna, or
- Pumpkin Lasagna

Sides
- Warm French Lentil Salad
- Crunchy Cauliflower with capers

Sweets
- Apple Raisin Bread
  (with vanilla gelato)
- Biscotti

Wine: Amarone

Appetizers
- Roasted Curried Corn Chowder
- Onion Bhaji

Main
- Aloo Gobi, or Indian Vegetable Curry

Sides
- Dal (with basmati rice)
- Cucumber Ginger Raita

Sweets
- Kheer
- Lisa's Coconut Pie

Wine: Riesling

SMALL PLATE PAIRINGS

I am a fan of small plates, for meals or for entertaining…

1. Baba Ghanoush
   Raita
   Dal
   Roasted Vegetable Mélange
   Onion Bhaji
   *Serve with warm naan and basmati rice
   Wine: Sancerre

2. Classic Stuffed Artichokes
   Minestrone Soup
   Classic Caesar Salad
   Pesto Stuffed Mushrooms
   *Serve with warm Italian semolina bread with sesame seeds
   Wine: Barbaresco

3. Potato Pancakes
   Cucumber Salad
   Wild Rice with Crunchy Tofu
   Stumble Upon Acorn Squash Soup
   Jeanne's Knækbrød
   Wine: Gewürztraminer

index

R

S

T

V

W

Y

Z

acknowledgments

Thank you to my greatest food guides, teachers and people who nourished me with so much love, through the food they made and in every other way. JoAnn Marengo, James Bassino, Eugenia Pagliaro Bassino, Deborah Bassino, Luciana Pisa Gheda, Nancy Mendelson, Tom Scott, Charlotte Devon Mendelson, Donald Charles Mendelson, and Lisa Gootee (of Coconut Pie fame). And thank you to my husband, Harley Flanagan, whom I adore, my stepsons Harley Karsten and Jonah Odin—my friends and family—all of whom I have the pleasure and privilege of feeding, and nourishing, and loving.

Hardcore Vegetarian: Welcome to the Vegedome!

ISBN: 9781934170953

PROCESS

Process Media
1240 W Sims Way #124
Port Townsend WA 98368
www.processmediainc.com
info@processmediainc.com

Designed by John Hubbard | emks.fi
Cover image by Ron Kretch
Back cover photo: Steve Joh

Printed in China